MW00444855

A GUIDE TO

Harriet Tubman's Eastern Shore

TO CATHERINE,

AN INTRODUCTION TO
HARRIET TUBMAN IN
APPRECIATION FOR YOUR
INTRODUCTION TO AUBURN,

SINCERELY,

7/1/22

A GUIDE TO

Harriet Tubman's Eastern Shore

THE OLD HOME IS NOT THERE

PHILLIP HESSER & CHARLIE EWERS

Foreword by Harriet Tubman biographer Kate Clifford Larson

THE
History
PRESS

Published by The History Press
Charleston, SC
www.historypress.com

Copyright © 2021 by Phillip Hesser and Charlie Ewers
All rights reserved

Front cover map and inset courtesy of the Library of Congress;
bottom and back cover images by Charlie Ewers.

First published 2021

Manufactured in the United States

ISBN 9781467149297

Library of Congress Control Number: 2021937069

Notice: The information in this book is true and complete to the best of our knowledge. It is
offered without guarantee on the part of the authors or The History Press. The authors and
The History Press disclaim all liability in connection with the use of this book.

All rights reserved. No part of this book may be reproduced or transmitted in any form
whatsoever without prior written permission from the publisher except in the case of brief
quotations embodied in critical articles and reviews.

Contents

Contents

Foreword

The history and memory of a place embody the physical and spiritual inheritance of the ordinary people who once lived there. When we look for their stories, we find them expressed through a brilliant patchwork of colors and subtle hues woven together in a complicated and intricate pattern of shared heritage. It informs what we think about ourselves and who we are. It can also inspire us.

Susan Wilson Photos.

In my many journeys to Harriet Ross Tubman's "homeplace" during more than two decades of research and collaboration on projects interpreting, imagining and sharing her remarkable life story, I have come to love and cherish these Eastern Shore landscapes where generations of her family lived, loved and survived. These fields and forests, rivers and marshes, roads and byways bore witness to numberless acts of everyday courage and resistance against immovable oppression. Every time I walk these grounds, I feel and see something different that informs my understanding of Tubman's remarkable fortitude and pluck.

I met Phil Hesser many years ago during the annual Harriet Tubman Underground Railroad Conference, held in Cambridge, Maryland, every June. He gave a brilliant and moving presentation on Tubman and her dreams, which he saw rooted in the physical and spiritual landscapes of her life. I sat riveted in my chair. In all my years studying Tubman, I had never contemplated the *meaning* of those dreams, nor their *roots.* Described by Tubman in private moments with her friends, in public to adoring audiences or remembered in sessions with early biographers, those dreams revealed how deeply imbedded those landscapes were to her physical, emotional and spiritual essence. I am forever grateful for Phil's insight and vision.

A Guide to Harriet Tubman's Eastern Shore: The Old Home Is Not There is a treat and a treasure. Illustrated by the evocative photographs of Charlie

Courtesy Kate Clifford Larson.

Ewers and interpreted with testimonies from people across the Eastern Shore who have connected in their own way with Tubman's "native land," it will sweep you across those landscapes—some physically transformed over two hundred years of human occupation and climate change, some remarkably whole—through a rich visual and textual journey of history and memory of Tubman's years as an enslaved person and young freedom fighter. You will see and feel her spirit rise up, gather energy and strike out for freedom and justice.

I hope it inspires you. I know it inspired me.

—KATE CLIFFORD LARSON, PhD
Author, Bound for the Promised Land: Harriet Tubman, Portrait of an American Hero

Preface

In the center of Harriet Tubman's landscape, the Legacy Garden of the Harriet Tubman Underground Railroad Visitor Center in Dorchester County, Maryland, is a quiet and scenic place for reflection on Tubman's life in her native land. *Charlie Ewers*.

She said she felt like a man who was put in State Prison for twenty-five years. All these twenty-five years he was thinking of his home, and longing for the time when he would see it again. At last the day comes—he leaves the prison gates—he makes his way to his old home, but his old home is not there. The house has been pulled down, and a new one has been put up in its place; his family and friends are gone nobody knows where; there is no one to take him by the hand, no one to welcome him.

—Sarah Hopkins Bradford, *Scenes in the Life of Harriet Tubman*, 1869

Harriet Tubman understood how the passing of time can rip apart the fabric of communities and landscapes—especially in her home state of Maryland that was so open to change, both political and environmental. She witnessed how her own family had been torn beyond repair in the matter of a decade or so as hundreds of enslaved people were "sold south" or struck out for freedom to the north. She also knew how lands close to bays and rivers big and small could be assaulted by tides, wind and water—flooding, washing away or sinking. She saw that buildings and other human modifications to the landscape required continual upkeep or fell to pieces when roofs rotted; walls tumbled down; and dams, ditch banks and canals washed in.

Walking along a path in the Legacy Garden of the Harriet Tubman Underground Railroad Visitor Center in Dorchester County, Maryland, a person who knows the landscape may note that the old house that once stood beside this property is no longer there. Hog Range, built by William Alvin Linthicum between 1910 and 1915, replaced an earlier house built by his uncle Captain Richard Linthicum III. Although identifying themselves as farmers in the late 1800s census records, the Linthicums—as was the case with their neighbor Lazarus Powell, who owned a steam-powered lumber mill with his son-in-law where the highway bridge now crosses the Blackwater River—made money harvesting and shipping logs for use as pilings and bridge timbers for a growing United States. Following in the footsteps of Harriet Tubman, African American neighbors of the Powells and Linthicums also forged a livelihood in the timber business at that time,

dragging logs to the docks with their teams of steers or cutting and carting cordwood for stoves and steam engines.

Forest products are still important in this part of Dorchester County, but visitors to the site are seeking not timber, but meaning. They come to learn more about a prominent figure in U.S. history and may know that she played a role in many of the principal human rights movements of the modern age, including abolition, civil rights, women's rights, rights of the elderly and rights of the disabled. About how this person struggled to obtain those rights for herself and secure them for others. About how this person was born and came of age in the landscape that surrounds the Legacy Garden.

If you have talked with the rangers in the Visitor Center, you most likely have learned that this site is the center point for Harriet Tubman's life in Dorchester County. To the east, across the Blackwater National Wildlife Refuge, you will first pass the farms where she kept house, tended children,

ABOVE: "The house has been pulled down and a new one has been put up in its place." Harriet Tubman Underground Railroad Visitor Center, adjacent to the site of Hog Range, the former Linthicum home, no longer standing. *Charlie Ewers.*

OPPOSITE: The trails of the Legacy Garden offer views that draw the eye to the marshes and Blackwater River to the south and the woods and the orientation of the Visitor Center toward freedom to the north. *Charlie Ewers.*

ABOVE: Harriet Tubman would have seen many ruined homes in her youth, often the result of families, free and enslaved, being torn apart or dispersed by a changing economy, debt and—in the case of enslaved people—being "sold south." *Charlie Ewers.*

learned to weave and trapped muskrats. Continuing in the same direction, you will reach the farm of the young man who claimed most of her family as his property. A bit farther in that direction, you will come to the location of a store where her preventing an overseer from abusing another enslaved person resulted in an injury that she would live with for the rest of her life. Even farther along, you will cross several roads and paths that led to Delaware and the free state of Pennsylvania.

To the west and north, away from the highway, you can follow roads or imagine footpaths or a "water trail" that would take you to Harriet Tubman's birthplace in Peter's Neck, the woods she harvested along Stewart's Canal and the sawmills and shipyards of Madison, the town once known as Tobacco Stick. In either direction, you might find churches she may have attended in the balconies designated for free and enslaved African Americans, worshipping with congregations of the people who owned most of this land and claimed ownership of the enslaved people who worked it and made it productive. You might also pass sites that were the scenes of annual camp meetings—also segregated—and of African American outdoor worship services and "bush meetings" in clearings that would later be adorned with Methodist Episcopal, Methodist Protestant and African Methodist Episcopal churches.

These sites have much to tell you about the details of Harriet Tubman's life and experiences, but they may reveal less about themselves. They reveal little about how they looked in Harriet Tubman's time. They only hint at how they offered home and livelihood to enslaved and free alike. They only whisper about how they have changed over nearly two centuries of modernizing agriculture, rising waters, clear-cut woods, sinking lands and species appearing, disappearing and reappearing.

❧

THIS BOOK is our way of telling the stories of these sites, employing the accounts of Harriet Tubman's early life as a skeleton key for unlocking a door into nineteenth-century Dorchester County. We do this first by connecting modern pictures of the site with the historical sources of Harriet Tubman's life—often in her own words. Second, we offer additional accounts or pictures—often from the nineteenth century—that help to add meaning to those stories. Finally, we hear from people from (or well acquainted with)

Dorchester County who have found meaning today in these landscapes related to Harriet Tubman's life and their own.

In using this "four-dimensional" point of view through the three dimensions of space and through time, we hope that readers will gain more from their experience following in the footsteps of Harriet Tubman in her native land. We hope that they will use their imaginations to think back in time, registering not only the inhumane treatment of enslaved persons in an often harsh landscape but also the power of faith, love and community to keep body and soul together—often across the miles of this landscape—in the worst of circumstances. This imaginary voyage through time can be simultaneously painful and edifying.

⤸

ULTIMATELY, by their going through this imaginary itinerary in time and space, we hope that people will take stock of the present through their reflections about the current landscape. In noting how things have changed in the nearly two hundred years since Harriet Tubman's birth, we can see where they have not. The global eradication of slavery would be a proud benchmark—if it were not dampened by its flaring up under the Islamic State and its smoldering beneath the surface in international human trafficking. The "liberating" nature of modern industrial and information technology could be a cause of celebration but is tempered with the effects of greenhouse gases from fossil fuels, trash and byproducts from factories collecting in our waters and along our roadsides, and social isolation and rancor encouraged by our reliance on digital tablets and cell phones.

Moreover, the legacy of slavery and its successor Jim Crow, while expunged from our law books, has not disappeared in the family memory and life experience of many. If we could imagine Harriet Tubman traveling in time to the twenty-first century, we certainly could imagine her troubled by hate crimes, angered at the shootings of African American men and women in travesties of community policing, outraged by continued human trafficking, shocked at the drowning lands around the Blackwater River, disgusted by the wasteful accumulations of plastic on the water and in landfills and saddened by people who treat others with indifference or hatred in social media. At the same time, she would be understanding of such change, remembering that twenty-five years can wear down a house and scatter the family that once lived there. She also would recall that a few short years could produce a turning point for humanity, bringing down a centuries-old institution such as slavery.

∽

MARGARET ATWOOD wrote that publishing a book is akin to stuffing a note into a bottle and throwing it into the sea—not knowing whether it will sink or float or, if it is found, whether it will be cherished, misinterpreted or "understood all too well by those who hate the message." We are cognizant of people who may wish to interpret our account as "cultural appropriation," defined by a 1992 resolution of the Writers' Union of Canada as "taking, from a culture that is not one's own, intellectual property, cultural expressions and artifacts, history and ways of knowledge." This observation might be made by a wide range of people whom we do not represent—natives of Dorchester County, African Americans, women, those with disabilities and others. We would argue, however, that the history of the civilizations of the world has been marked by borrowings that often have advanced human understanding and progress. Moreover, cross-boundary and cross-cultural accounts of human experience have gained in translation when backed up by sound and enlightening historical research in archives and other keys to our past. Our world would be considerably different—and less rich in ideas—if nations or people appreciated and researched only their own intellectual property and culture.

In addition, we recognize with people of color what Lynell George of the *Los Angeles Times* in 1994 called "the sting of having their stories half-told, mis-told, or told for the profit of others, if at all." As for telling the stories, we note that we have taken accounts of Harriet Tubman's life in her native land of Dorchester that were in the public domain, recounted to the public by Harriet Tubman herself and long available to people she hoped would learn from them. In contrast, we have not sought to extract stories that may yet lie in the personal possession of people of color, of women or of elderly or disabled people who cherish community or family memories, nor have we attempted to draw from cultural lore or deep-seated appreciation of Harriet Tubman. We hope that these communities would share these stories with the rest of us in a way that respects their telling and their context.

In many ways, we have tried to aspire to what filmmaker, composer, educator and deep reader Trinh T. Minh-ha has termed "speaking nearby rather than talking about." She describes this as "a speaking that does not objectify, does not point to an object as if it is distant from the speaking subject or absent from the speaking place. A speaking that reflects on itself and can come very close to a subject without, however, seizing or claiming it." We have tried not to objectify Harriet Tubman and others in her native land, but to reflect on what we have heard in reading the words committed to her life and to draw near to her, while respecting the space she has created with her narrative.

As for the profit question, we note that the authors' proceeds from the sale of this book will go to Friends of the Harriet Tubman Visitor Center to be used to fund its programs of cultural and historical appreciation. In other words, we hope that people will receive this book as a contribution in ideas and resources to a worthwhile public enterprise.

Finally, we agree with the distinction offered by bell hooks in 1990 that "there's a significant difference between cultural appropriation and cultural appreciation." The story of Harriet Tubman has been appreciated by listeners and readers since at least 1855. It has been retold by many people of goodwill—white and Black, male and female, writers and journalists, historians, reenactors and novelists, old and young, those with disabilities and those without. Hers is a story that is universal. As such, it has called out to people to tell it to their generation, to make it echo in their world. Although her being treated as chattel is something that could be fully appreciated in our day only by people enslaved by so-called holy war or by human trafficking, her suffering and abuse—even after slavery was abolished—saddens all of us more than a century after her death. Her prevailing despite the odds and seeing to the happiness of others gives every one of us cause to hope and to act.

⚮

WE APPRECIATE that the quotations we draw from the Harriet Tubman biographies may prove difficult to our readers in more than one way. At the very least, they can be challenging to read, given the attempts to reproduce dialect. More importantly, they reflect an effort by white writers who quote Harriet Tubman to lace her language with their interpretation of Black voices and expression.

This issue remains a painful one in our day. In November 2020, as this book was going to press, Dr. Regina N. Bradley, assistant professor of English and African Diaspora Studies and writer and researcher of African American life, witnessed her essay "Da Art of Speculatin" (a play on OutKast's "Da Art of Storytellin'") interpreted in an audio version by a white man attempting to read the essay with his take on an accent not his own.

Dr. Bradley responded in a tweet, "WHAT THE HELL IS THIS?!?! This is what you think I'd sound like?" She denounced this narration as "this minstrel take" and added, "To have my truth taken from me and minstrelized is just…." She returned to the subject again by describing herself as "being at the center of a minstrelsy performance." Other commenters agreed, calling the expropriation of her voice "19th century racist," "*awful.* Minstrel-sounding jokey nonsense," "auditory blackface" and a "gross caricature."

We have considered the language and dialect used in the quotes of Harriet Tubman by several white authors for their veering into "jokey ministrelsy" or—at the very least—obscuring her words in a cloud of seeming Black speech. Yet, when faced with the possibility of editing these quotes, we have decided in favor of leaving the quotes as they are, a testimony to what her white biographers chose to record in their time. To do otherwise would compound the distortion of speaking on behalf of Harriet Tubman.

We believe that these words as formulated by her white biographers in the era of minstrelsy speak for themselves. Nonetheless, the words harken back to what was said by Harriet Tubman, reflecting her faith, her sense of humor and her truth-telling. For all those reasons, they are faithfully quoted for the reader to reflect on as one more distant, but revealing, aspect of her life.

Our readers will notice that we have not edited the N-word in the quotations from Harriet Tubman's native land. We have chosen not to do this knowing that the question of standards has challenged public platforms in recent years. In 2016, Shaun King, a senior justice writer for the *New York Daily News*, had his Facebook account blocked for twenty-four hours because he had violated Facebook "Community Standards." The cause of this violation was his quoting a hate message he had received using the N-word. Once Facebook was "alerted to the mistake," it restored the post and apologized. According to Facebook's current policy, "We allow the content but expect people to clearly indicate their intent."

Our intent is to quote the sources and employ the visuals as they were published so that the reader will see the implicit brutality of words and sometimes images employed by white writers in the nineteenth and twentieth centuries. These words and images of the past need to be called out, just as Shaun King called out the hate message addressed to him in the present. In doing this, we hope that our readers will recognize these words and images for what they are: steeped in the racism of the period before abolition, attached to the rhetoric of race in the Jim Crow era and unfortunately lingering in our age of universal human rights.

ول

IN TELLING her parable about the former prisoner who returns to his birthplace to find that the old home is not there, Harriet Tubman adds that a new house has been built in its place, further compounding the sense of forlornness felt by the prisoner. This image brings us into contact with another kind of appropriation—that of ownership or mastery of the environment or a landscape—to which we have been sensitive in preparing this book.

The posts or fences that established the boundaries of the landowners of Harriet Tubman's native land also marked their authority over the enslaved people they legally owned and whose movements they often restricted to their property lines. Other forms of appropriation can be seen as that of enslaved people over the land legally owned by the people at whose order the posts were sunk and the fences were built. In this case, enslaved people—often in secret—mastered the land for their own purposes and survival; gathering additional food, medicine or commodities; and traveling on hidden paths in secret to come together as a family, to worship or to escape.

Yet another form of landscape or environmental appropriation can be seen in any human effort to impose a regime on nature. The men and women who claimed ownership or mastery of Harriet Tubman also claimed

FOLLOWING, TOP: This photograph of an access road north and west of World's End Creek on Maryland State Highway 336 shows the signage of Blackwater National Wildlife Refuge "staking out" its possession of this narrow corridor with signs. *Charlie Ewers.*

FOLLOWING, BOTTOM: This view of the Brodess Farm historical site shows how landscape is marked off and appropriated by those with rights to the property. In this case, the area on the right is public for historical interpretation with signs and parking. The area to the left behind the gates and fence is private—to be respected by the public. *Charlie Ewers.*

FOLLOWING, FULL: The dying loblolly pines of a "ghost forest" along the upper Blackwater River are witnesses to the sinking land, rising sea level and flushing of the tidal waters. *Charlie Ewers.*

large tracts of land to be cleared of timber for lumber and boats, ditched and diked for reclaimed land, planted with crops or enclosed for livestock, harvested for its animal or plant life and in some places burned on a regular basis to do these things. Harriet Tubman did some of these things herself, at the orders of the people who claimed her labor or hired her out. She did them to nurse herself or her loved ones. She did them to earn money. She did them to escape or help others escape to freedom.

From what we know of her life in her native land, she did these things in what we would call "low impact" ways today, such as using steers to bring out individual logs from a forest. Others in her time might have had a greater impact—destroying land cover by clearing forests, silting in creeks by breaking up soil through plowing, exposing land to erosion by digging canals and upsetting patterns of fish spawning by building dams. Technology has added to the reach of the people living today in Harriet Tubman's native land with machines that can clear-cut the woods and, in the process, add greenhouse gases to contribute to climate change.

We have noted throughout this book where Harriet Tubman's native land has changed well beyond her recognition through the flooding and swelling of the once-curving banks of the Blackwater and Little Blackwater Rivers and the washing back and forth of tides along the Blackwater from Stewart's Canal to the north to Fishing Bay to the south. And so, through this book, we have appropriated the landscape and the environment as a tool for teaching and reflection. Yet if its readers gain perspective and appreciation from the stories told by the landscapes of these sites, as they do from the accounts of the scenes of Harriet Tubman's Dorchester years, we will have turned that appropriation to good ends.

⁂

HARRIET TUBMAN used her parable of the prisoner to describe how she felt when she crossed the line into freedom alone for the first time in her life. Acknowledging that the rest of her life would be different, she would remedy this alienation through connections that supported abolitionism, brought other people out of slavery, contributed to the Union war effort, took part in the women's suffrage movement, provided a home for the elderly and disabled and lived a life according to her faith and values. It is our hope that finding meaning in Harriet Tubman's native land—in envisioning her nineteenth-century life and landscape and in appreciating her courage and vision in that setting—will encourage visitors to reflect in the Legacy Garden and inside the Visitor Center and to explore how values, vision and determination can transcend historical experience and environmental change. The old home is not there, but its story can inform, caution and inspire.

—PHILLIP HESSER

Acknowledgements

T his project has benefited from many people from its inception through the many months of exploring landscapes and the stories that infuse them. First, our appreciation goes out to our interviewees, whose contributions are showcased throughout these pages and who "brought home" our account to their own experiences with Harriet Tubman's native land or the activities that were an important part of her life: Ted Abbott, Dion Banks, Kate Bradshaw, Tom Bradshaw, Ruth Braxton, Rene Campbell, Kimerly Cornish, Angela Crenshaw, the late Linda Duyer, Amanda Fenstermaker, Shirlyn Henry Brown, Scott Holnikner, Shirley Jackson, Victoria Jackson-Stanley, William Jarmon, Herschel Johnson, Bertha Mack, Steve Matthias, Jay Meredith, Susan Meredith, Gary L. Moore, Kisha Petticolas, Donald Pinder, David Pletcher, Clara Small, Brice Stump, Marvel Travis, Joanne Morvay Weant and Dornell L. Woolford.

We offer our thanks to the people of the many programs that interpret Harriet Tubman's native land or the institutions or activities of her early life in Dorchester: William Jarmon, the Harriet Tubman Organization; Ray Paterra and Bill Giese, Blackwater National Wildlife Refuge; Barb Duffin and Philip Lawton, Barratt's Chapel & Museum of Methodism; Grace Tartaglia, Furnace Town Historic Site; Steve Matthias, Scott Holniker and Joanne Morvay Weant, Carroll County Farm Museum; David Pletcher and Marilee Pletcher, Stahlstown Flax Scutching Festival; Daniel Dunlap, Old Trinity Church; Creston Long and Donna Messick, Edward H. Nabb

Research Center for Delmarva History and Culture at Salisbury University; Eileen McHugh of the Cayuga Museum of History and Art (for the Emma Telford manuscript *Harriet: The Modern Moses of Heroism and Visions*); and Dion Banks and Kisha Petticolas, Eastern Shore Network for Change. We likewise thank the people who took the time to read our draft manuscript and make suggestions: Angela Crenshaw, Kate Clifford Larson, Dana Paterra, Clara Small, G. Ray Thompson and Dornell L. Woolford.

We also express our thanks to those who assisted us with the scans and rights to historical images that help to tell our story: Dion Banks for the photo of the Harriet Tubman Ambulance from the photo album of his grandmother Evelyn Jones-Banks; Sam Bessen of the Lester S. Levy Sheet Music Collection of the Sheridan Libraries of Johns Hopkins University; Tricia Gesner of Associated Press; Larry Hardy of the *Times & Democrat*, Orangeburg, South Carolina; Edwin L. Jackson from his photography collection as featured in Georgia Studies Images; Maryland Department of Natural Resources; Ming Li of the Horn Point Lab of the University of Maryland Center for Environmental Science; Taylor L. Reynolds of Delaware Public Archives; and Barbara J. Seese of Dorchester Center for the Arts.

To the organizations and their representatives who gave us the opportunity to give talks related to this book, we wish to give a shout out: Diane Miller, national program manager, National Underground Railroad Network to Freedom, National Park Service, for inviting us to the 2019 Niagara Falls Underground Railroad Training; College English Association–Middle Atlantic Group, for the opportunity to give the keynote address to the Annual Spring Conference, "Tides & Surges"; and Jack Hirschfeld, vice president, Havre de Grace Arts Collective, for the chance to deliver the address for the Weekend Celebrating Harriet Tubman and the Underground Railroad in February 2020.

We wish to single out a few people who informed and supported this project from the beginning and throughout its long gestation:

- *Angela Crenshaw and Dana Paterra, Maryland Department of Natural Resources, who read proof-of-concept chapters, shared their feelings about Harriet Tubman's landscape and looked and commented on the entire manuscript;*
- *Joseph F. diPaolo, who shared manuscripts and the learnings of his several books on the early history of Methodism;*
- *Kimerly Cornish, who introduced us—as she has many through her talks and writings—to critical perspectives that help us to do justice to Harriet Tubman's legacy, fulfilling her sacred trust as a member of the Ross family;*

- *G. Ray Thompson, who reviewed the manuscript and also shared his long acquaintance with Delmarva history and archival resources in helping us to get a better feel for the landscape of the mid-nineteenth century;*
- *Kate Clifford Larson, author and educator, whose Tubman biography* Bound for the Promised Land *has introduced so many of us to the person at the center of our landscape, for sharing her considerable talents through reading, correcting, commenting, mentoring and writing the foreword to this book, a product that would be nearly unthinkable if it were not for her encouragement; and*
- *Kate Jenkins, acquisitions editor; Abigail Fleming, production editor; and Hilary Parrish, proofreader, with Arcadia Publishing/The History Press, who have shepherded this book (and its authors) insightfully and gently through publication.*

Finally, we wish to acknowledge our gratitude and appreciation to our spouses, Nancy G. Hesser and Theo Ewers. They have accompanied us on many miles of the roads through Harriet Tubman's native land and have the insect bites to show for it. Their patience and encouragement have blessed us to the last mile of the odyssey that we now present to the reader.

Introduction

When I think of home, I think of a place
Where there's love overflowing
I wish I was home, I wish I was back there
With the things I've been knowing.

—"Home," from *The Wiz*, Charlie Smalls, composer/lyricist

For Harriet Tubman, Dorchester County, Maryland, had to be a vexing place, fraught with paradoxes: a place where family lived and family was stolen, life-giving and life-draining, expansive and constrictive. Still, it was familiar. So it is no wonder that in Benjamin Drew's *A North-side View of Slavery*, she reflected, "We [formerly enslaved people] would rather stay in our native land, if we could be free there as we are here." But as the law of the land did not recognize her humanity and right to freedom, Harriet had to set up literal homes away from the place of her birth—in St. Catharines, Canada, and ultimately Auburn in central New York. The one constant in all of those homes was her family. For Harriet Tubman, her family was her home.

In most dictionaries, the first definition of the word *home* refers to a physical place. But for the enslaved, dispossessed of homeland, liberty and their very humanity, another conception of home had to be created as a matter of survival. In "Homeplace (A Site of Resistance)," bell hooks articulates this notion of home. She writes:

The task of making homeplace was not simply a matter of black women providing service; it was about the construction of a safe place where black people could affirm one another and by so doing heal many of the wounds inflicted by racist domination. We could not learn to love or respect ourselves in the culture of white supremacy, on the outside; it was there on the inside, "in that homeplace," most often created and kept by black women that we had the opportunity to grow and develop, to nurture our spirits.[1]

An examination of Harriet Tubman's life bears out this more abstract definition of home. It is also telling that most of the persons she was documented to have rescued were family and friends. Her knowledge of the people, the land and the habits of life in Dorchester County contributed to her success as a conductor on the Underground Railroad. For instance, Harriet could draw on her knowledge of the healing properties of plants like cranesbill and water lilies to treat maladies on the long, arduous journey to freedom.

In recent years, as another native daughter of Dorchester County, I have made the trip from central New York to home many times myself, though my journeys were not perilous as Harriet's were. During my time as an undergraduate at Oberlin College, there were regular trips home and care packages of food that only someone from the Eastern Shore would appreciate. Because of the time I spent in Oberlin, Ohio, a location known to be a junction on several Underground Railroad routes and in central New York, I have triangulated the Underground Railroad, nearly 150 years after Harriet first used the network to liberate so many. While I've always had an appreciation for the unique culture of Dorchester County, my affinity for the land is what has grown most as a direct result of Harriet Tubman's story, which is inextricably tied to the natural history of the region.

I cannot claim an ounce of the knowledge that enabled Harriet's survival and ultimate escape to freedom. The diversity and multitude of plants and wildlife of which she had understanding cannot be underestimated, especially since some may no longer be as plentiful as in her time. As a child, I remember fondly crabbing and fishing with my father. I also remember the mosquitoes—so overwhelming one year that the school-aged kids engaged

---

1. In *Yearning: Race, Gender and Cultural Politics*, 1999, 42.

in a letter-writing campaign to Governor Harry Hughes for relief. Today, I wonder what Harriet's remedy would have been in the same situation. She wasn't intimidated by the vastness of the unspoiled, undeveloped landscape in her time, as I have been in mine. She leveraged her wisdom to effect freedom for herself and others. It was her unique gift: to take elements of her life that were considered deficits and turn them into assets. The "neglected weed" to which Harriet likened herself in her remarks in Drew's text was an apt botanical metaphor, highlighting her deep connection to and understanding of the natural world. Harriet's life of hard physical labor in the outdoors enabled her to explore and amass a deep reservoir of knowledge to aid her on her journey to freedom.

I was fortunate to have been born and raised in Dorchester County, so I learned about Harriet's legacy primarily from family and community members, not textbooks. Even before my mother, Betty Cornish, gave official tours of Harriet Tubman's Dorchester County, I remember vividly the unofficial tours I was given. We regularly visited family in south Dorchester. As with fishing and crabbing trips, the quiet of the country heightened the buzz of the native insects and other creatures. The unique south Dorchester ecosystem provided the soundtrack to family storytelling about kin long since passed and a way of life that had largely faded away. Unfortunately, during my formative years, I did not recognize that the oral tradition that documented my Harrisville Road family history was an integral part of the culture too and that it could disappear if not nurtured.

The discomfort and disconnection I felt in contemporary rural Dorchester County was nothing compared to what Harriet and other ancestors of the antebellum era felt. I have not known the pain of forced familial separation or the difficult decision to live free or die trying. It is in adulthood that I have come to see the lessons in those hardships. The country roads where I first learned to drive were once well-populated by indigenous animals and plants of which Harriet had encyclopedic knowledge that she drew on to survive and ultimately escape.

Harriet's story is a story of liberation and preservation. For Harriet, home was more than a location; it was people. At her last home in Auburn, New York, Harriet gathered her family on several acres and created a new homeplace. No doubt, in Harriet's Cayuga County, New York home, she used the skills she had honed in childhood and in that way kept a part of Dorchester County, Maryland, with her.

As family passes away and landmarks recede, it is challenging to preserve as much as possible of Harriet Tubman's legacy and her Dorchester County for future generations. We must be humble in our queries, recognize that we are looking with our modern-day eyes and attempt to see things as she saw them as well. Harriet's knowledge, faith and love guided her lifelong mission. She embodied the wisdom of ancestors like her grandmother Modesty. She passed on much of her wisdom orally to those who knew how to listen, as it was passed to her.

Sai Krishna Kumaraswamy.

After my mother died, I truly realized that history is not just in books; it resides in people and the stories they tell. To honor the work she and others in the community did when I was growing up, I continue in my own way to embody and transmit the history of Harriet Tubman and other ancestors and the indelible imprint they left on Dorchester County and the world.

—KIMERLY CORNISH
Educator
Collateral descendant, Ross family

1

The House Has Been Pulled Down

READING INTO A SITE IN THE NATIVE LAND OF HARRIET TUBMAN

The first site in Dorchester County to mark the life of Harriet Tubman in 1967, the Brodess Farm is an important stopping-off point for visiting Harriet Tubman's "native land." Although much has changed here since the days of her being enslaved by Edward Brodess, the site can help us to "read" the landscapes inhabited and mastered by Harriet Tubman in her formative years. *Charlie Ewers.*

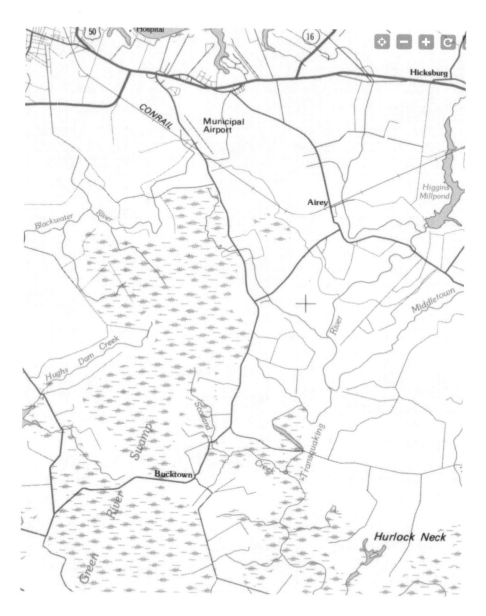

U.S. Soil Conservation Service, Dorchester County, Maryland, 1979. This map gives a bird's-eye view of the itinerary discussed in this chapter. *Library of Congress, Geography and Map Division.*

It weaves through a rare landscape,
virtually unaltered for more than a century.

—Harriet Tubman Underground Railroad Visitor Center, "Welcome Guide," 2017

To read the story of Harriet Tubman in her native land of Dorchester County, Maryland, leave aside the printed page and drive a little over nine miles on Bucktown Road, leaving US Highway 50 just south of Cambridge. Pass the Cambridge Airport and cross the tracks near the site of the Thompson station of the Dorchester and Delaware Railroad, built after Harriet Tubman's years in Dorchester. Continue beyond the left turn for Cordtown Road, where relatives of Tubman's husband settled and harvested timber in the nineteenth century. Expect to weave back and forth on a

Bucktown United Methodist Church, also known as Scott's Chapel for Henry Scott, who provided this property in 1812. *Charlie Ewers.*

country road that has been shaped by the property lines of farms, stands of timber and water courses.

For now, ignore the lanes branching to the left, such as Indian Bone Road, named for Native American remains found there. Slowing down as you reach the village of Bucktown, zigzag around what is left of a beaver pond and dam—the dam likely used as the base for a road crossing a creek that long ago offered access to the Transquaking River to the first inhabitants of the area. Arrive at the crossroads, where a store was the scene for a major event in Tubman's life. Turn right on Greenbrier Road for the site most deeply connected with Harriet Tubman.

BUCKTOWN

Is situated near the Transquaking river, 5 miles from Airey's, on the D. & D. R. R. Climate uniformly mild and healthy. Land medium; sells at from $8 to $20 per acre; produces 10 to 15 bus. wheat, 12 to 20 oats, 60 to 150 potatoes, 25 corn and 1+ tons hay. Public school, C. A. Lecompte, teacher. Population 20. J. B. Meredith, Postmaster.

General Merchandise. Holt, H, Meredith, J.B., Wall, J.B.

Trader. Willey, E. M.

Wheelwright. Wheatley, William

"Dorchester," *The Maryland Directory,* 1878

A mile or so beyond the Bucktown crossroads, turn to the left to enter the parking area for the Brodess Farm Site. Take a careful look at the landscape of the homeplace of Edward Brodess, who claimed ownership of the enslaved Harriet Tubman and her mother, sisters and brothers. As the first public site in Dorchester County to mark the Dorchester life of Harriet Tubman (in 1967), this place is a fitting spot to start to read the landscape of Harriet Tubman's native land.

In scanning the landscape of the Brodess Farm, avoid skimming over what you see. Instead, pause a moment to take in all of the images, recognizing that they are largely modern. Expand on them and visualize their past with your mind's eye. Add to them with your other senses and project what you see, smelling and hearing Harriet Tubman's native land of the early and mid-nineteenth century.

In short, use your imagination to scroll back to the time of Harriet Tubman. What would she have seen, heard, smelled, tasted and felt nearly two centuries ago? In what ways can you make your vision of the past similar to what she experienced? In what ways have things changed in nearly two centuries?

The property had areas of dense pines almost too dense to walk through. Other sections had trees 20 to 30 feet tall. Still others had not been timbered

ABOVE: The Brodess Farm fronting Greenbrier Swamp, the source of legends and of valuable resources for people living in the area. *Charlie Ewers.*

LEFT: *Harriet Tubman Underground Railroad Byway Driving Tour Map, Site 16.*

in 50 years. In these last areas, the pines stood 50 to 60 feet tall without branches for the first 40 feet. The underbrush had all been killed by the shade, and the high, green branches at the top gave a cathedral effect above a rich carpet of pine needles.

Honeysuckle, blackberries and huckleberries grew along the edges of the clearings in these woods, but no grass or weeds grew under the cathedral pines although several varieties of orchids called lady's slippers could be found where the sunlight was sufficient.

—P.J. Wingate, "I Remember…Cutting Loblolly Pine as a Youth in Dorchester," (Baltimore) *Sun*, October 19, 1969

As you would look at a landscape painting or photograph, size up the background. Looking south from the parking area, you will see a field framed by a backdrop of trees. These trees front Greenbrier Swamp, a part of which was still owned by the Brodess family in the day of Harriet Tubman. Although some of the original oak and other hardwood trees may have been standing in the early nineteenth century, much of the area had likely been cut for any usable timber and overgrown with loblolly or "old field" pine. In the wetter areas, gum, maple, beech, holly and cedar trees would have grown. Although Greenbrier Swamp must have teemed with stories and legends that would have scared the younger folk especially, it would have been a treasure-trove for all of the people of the area for hunting, trapping and gathering of firewood, berries, roots and herbs.

In addition to footpaths connecting sections of higher ground, there likely would have been skid roads (shallow gullies etched into the landscape in and out of the swamp), where teamsters drove mules and steers (oxen) to harvest the remaining hardwood trees and second-growth pines—an important source of wood for furniture and household items, as well as for cordwood, the major source of fuel for heating and cooking.

As the sun fades, a mist droops over Green Briar Swamp [sic]. *In the gathering gloom it creeps toward the woods snaking through dense underbrush and slithers across fields. The air grows heavy. Silent. The farmlands bordering Green Briar Swamp seem to shiver under mid-summer stars. Throaty moans of frogs squatting in slime around the fringes of the*

OPPOSITE: Greenbrier Swamp today may reflect how it looked at the time of Harriet Tubman, following logging with the first wave of settlers. *Charlie Ewers.*

marsh are the only sounds to penetrate the shrouded silence of night taut as a bowstring....Night swallows the swamp and the farmland that borders it with forbidding blackness. The ghosts of Green Briar prowl undisturbed.

—Brice Stump, *A Visit with the Past*, 1968

Your thoughts about what could be found in Harriet Tubman's day and what was hearsay in Greenbrier Swamp might not be limited to ghost stories and legends. You would not find the larger animals found there a generation or two before. Bears, beavers and deer would have been hunted out for their furs, skins, meat and other valuable products. Wolves would have been killed for the bounties on their heads. Foxes, skunks and opossums, however, would

ABOVE: The Dorchester marshes and the watercourses that flow through them long have been a valuable resource for the people of the area. Trappers, waterfowlers, turtle catchers and fishermen/women have made a living and provided for the table—especially in the cold months when they could not work the land. *Charlie Ewers.*

OPPOSITE, TOP: An important source of feed for the Delmarva poultry industry, soybeans date back in Dorchester to the middle part of the twentieth century. *Charlie Ewers.*

OPPOSITE, BOTTOM: Following its introduction to the southern and midwestern United States in the late nineteenth century, milo (a variety of sorghum) spread to Maryland in the mid-twentieth century for its use as "chicken corn," a component of poultry feed. These fields would have been as strange to Harriet Tubman in mid-nineteenth-century Dorchester County as the soybeans seen in the previous photograph. *Charlie Ewers.*

be there to stage their rounds around the farm at night and squirrels and rabbits by day. Just beyond the Brodess Farm, muskrats (a familiar sight to Harriet Tubman, which she trapped as a girl) would be trapped in winter in their lodges on the marshes along the Transquaking River and its tributaries. Mice and rats would be found at the farm in the barns and likely in the houses.

Your wanderings through the swamp and along the water courses might bring you into contact with snakes, including copperheads and a variety of black snakes. On a summer day, your footsteps might flush a toad from its cover in the shade, and your ears at night would ring with the calling of hundreds of frogs after a rain. In the warmer months of the year, you might encounter a terrapin or snapping turtle—a welcome addition to the stewpot.

The sights and sounds of birds would be quite different in your visioning of the past. You would not see the house sparrow, which would have been introduced from Britain to New York about the time when Harriet Tubman left Dorchester County. Instead, you would see familiar cardinals, woodpeckers, mockingbirds, blackbirds, crows, bald eagles, doves, robins, hawks, buzzards, ospreys and—in season—ducks and geese on their migrations. In the day, you also would have seen bluebirds and heard whippoorwills at night. The turkeys you see today in the area are from birds introduced a century ago.

In addition to today's mosquitoes and ticks, several forms of biting flies, including—not surprisingly for the horse and buggy age—horseflies, would have bedeviled the people here. By day, honeybees would have been quite common, whether in the wild or in farm hives. By night, fireflies would have been seen in the fields in summer.

As you look across the foreground from the parking area and even around you across the road, take in the fields that testify to the land's productivity. Depending on the season, you might see corn or wheat, familiar crops in the nineteenth century. Now, however, you might see soybeans instead, a crop introduced here in the mid-twentieth century. Whatever the case, you are seeing the broad fields of a single crop grown with farm machinery to meet the needs of the century-old chicken industry or even for international trade. In fact, the Brodess Farm is only one of several large tracts in the area now owned by Blackwater Farms Inc.

Should it chance to be early summer, the rolling surface presents its slopes on every side clothed in varied shades of green. Here the rich hue of the waving wheat-fields, broken by long lines of lighter coloring where the young oat-crop fills in the rows on which the corn was stacked in autumn; there the deeper hue of the heavy-leaved maize, blue and succulent in its luxuriant growth—the handsomest crop which a farmer's gaze can rest on; yonder a herd of lazy cattle knee-deep amid the purple bloom of the clover, or a broad expanse of fresh orchard foliage giving promise of ripened sweetness under the glowing kisses of the sun. The farm-houses, one or more of which will always be in sight, have an air of thrift and of substantial comfort, the large barns giving evidence of the expectation, at least, of full crops, and the sleek pigs and fat poultry bearing testimony to the realization of such hopes. Few of these houses are of modern style, while many of them are the long, small-windowed, porchless brick dwellings of a century ago.

—Robert Wilson, "On the Eastern Shore," *Lippincott's Magazine*, July 1876

VENDUE

The subscriber, as administrator of Levin W. Stewart, will sell at public sale, at his late residence, Tobaccostick.

On Tuesday, Sept. 15, 1857,

A great variety of the PERSONAL ESTATE of the said deceased, consisting of Furniture in the house, Farming Utensils, including two wheat reapers, one Drill, Corn Shellers, Wheat Fan; one Carriage, crop of Corn on the ground, a large number of valuable Cattle, Sheep, Hogs, some excellent Horses, Mules, &c., one-half of the schooner "MANSION," about two years old, and carrying some 140 tons, and a large lot of Clover Hay.

Terms as usual and made known specifically on the day of sale,

JAMES A. STEWART
Administrator,
September 2, 1857

(Dorchester) *Democrat,* September 2, 1857

Vendue (sale) notices in the local papers give us a good idea of what might be found on a farm of the period. James A. Stewart, the administrator, was the brother of the deceased and of John T. Stewart, to whom Harriet Tubman had hired out her time.

Rewinding in your imagination to Harriet Tubman's day would bring you to quite a different set of fields nestled between the stands of trees and Greenbrier Road. The *Maryland Directory* for 1878—later than Harriet Tubman's Dorchester years, but likely still accurate for her time—speaks of crops of wheat, oats, potatoes, corn and hay. These would have been grown at the same time or in rotation in smaller plantings that could be tended by horse- or mule-drawn plows driven by farm laborers. In addition, the Brodess Farm likely grew flax (which Harriet Tubman remembers "breaking" for its fiber to weave into clothing when she was hired out to another family). Grapevines, berry canes and fruit and nut trees may have

ABOVE: Currier & Ives, *American Farm Yard—Evening*, circa 1857. This illustration shows many of the animals that would be found at the Brodess Farm in Harriet Tubman's day. Missing are the mules, steers and sheep common to mid-nineteenth-century Dorchester County. *Library of Congress.*

OPPOSITE: The one-story section of Meredith House, adjacent to the Bucktown General Store, was probably built before the two-story section of the later nineteenth century and may reflect a farmhouse style adopted by Anthony Thompson to build for his stepson, Edward Brodess. *Charlie Ewers.*

grown on the property, and people on the farm would have their own gardens for vegetables, beans, peas, herbs and fruit.

Imagine the assortment of domesticated animals that would have been raised on the farm. In addition to horses, mules or steers ploughing the fields or pulling wagons or dragging timber, a flock of chickens would have supplied eggs, sheep would have provided the wool for a pair of pants or a shawl, a cow or two would have provided milk and butter and hogs would have furnished meat. A mixed-breed dog or two might be seen resting in the shade of a house and several cats lounging near the barn. If you listen carefully, you might hear the jingle of a harness, a bark, a bleat or the crowing of a rooster. If you take a deep breath, you would smell the lingering woodsmoke from the fires used to cook breakfast or supper, to keep the home warm on a cool day or even to dispose of burnable trash. Depending on the direction of the wind, you might smell an outhouse a short walk from the farmhouse or a faint aroma of manure or the mire of the pigpen.

In the middle distance, imagine the farmhouse of the Brodess Farm. It would not be the house we see today, which appeared on the property in the early twentieth century. Instead, we would have seen something similar to the Chesapeake plantation described by Joseph Scott in his *Geographical Description of the State of Maryland* of 1810:

> *The planters towards the bay, build their houses upon some eminence, remote from the miasmata of the low marshy grounds, and stagnant waters. Their dwellings, in the counties on the Chesapeak [sic], are mostly of frame, generally painted brown or yellow. At a little distance from the dwellings of the planters, are the huts or quarters of their slaves.*

♂

> *I love thy moss-covered roof and pointed gables, thy ancient walls and dormer windows, thy lofty halls and wainscot ceiling, each nook and cranny, each closet and cupboard are near familiar spots.*

—William J. Leonard, diary, 1862. *This account, written in a Confederate prison during the Civil War, offers us an idealized view of Leonard's farm.*

This type of home is a far cry from the white-columned plantation houses of modern novels and films. According to court records, the home Anthony Thompson built for his stepson Edward Brodess was a "single story 32 by 20 [foot house with] two rooms below with plank floors and brick chimney and also a barn of good material." Quarters for the enslaved people of the Brodess Farm would have been a cluster of shed-like outbuildings located at the edge of the farm fields. On larger farms, there would have been a modest shanty for the farm overseer, such as the one who would be responsible for injuring Harriet Tubman at the Bucktown store.

Other buildings might have included a stable, icehouse (where ice harvested in winter was stored in pits filled with straw for insulation), milk house (a cellar where dairy items might be kept cooler), smokehouse (for preserving the family's meat), silos, barns, workshops, outhouse and pens for the pigs and sheep and coops for the roosting chickens. A well and a rain barrel would have provided water for the household and animals. Possibly the sweet or Irish potatoes grown on the farm would have been banked in a pit lined with straw

OPPOSITE, TOP: E.H. Pickering, "Farmhouse near Shrewsbury Church US 13, Locust Grove, Kent County, Maryland," post-1933. This design may reflect the original Brodess Farmhouse. *Library of Congress.*

OPPOSITE, BOTTOM: The remains of a store at Wesley in south Dorchester County. This survivor of a century ago reveals the basic design of a country store, often extended on both sides to make more room for inventory. *Charlie Ewers.*

and protected by a wood cover, where the cook could have picked through the straw to gather a few whenever they were needed for a meal.

Give or take the youngest children—white or Black—toddling near their homes, a normal day might have seen only a few people out and about. Would we have seen Edward Brodess looking about the farm and giving orders to his hands? Or would he have been preparing his horse to ride down the lane to go to town or visit his friends? Would we have seen his wife, Eliza, ordering a farmhand to bring more wood into the kitchen?

Likely we would have seen an enslaved cook or maid shuttling in and out of the house to fetch eggs, hang laundry or send a farmhand on an errand to a Bucktown store just over a mile away. Perhaps a free Black man or woman would come to the farm from down the Bestpitch Road with game, fish, terrapins, berries or a wood bowl or basket to sell. With the exception of special days bringing many people together for planting,

ABOVE: L.D. Andrew (reproduced from old photograph), "View in Kitchen, Refuge Plantation, Satilla River, Woodbine, Camden County, GA," n.d. Kitchen workers, such as Rit Ross (Harriet Tubman's mother) and the person depicted here, played key roles in the workings of a farm household. *Library of Congress.*

harvesting, threshing, raising a new building or slaughtering the hogs, we would hear only the faint hum of activity mixed with the cries and shouts of the youngest children, including Edward Brodess's eight sons and daughters, born from the 1820s to early 1840s.

Would we have seen Rit Ross, Harriet's mother? An accomplished cook, she may have been hired out to a neighbor for additional income to the Brodess household and could have stayed there for most of the year. Would we have seen Minty (as Harriet was known in her youth)? Hired out from her earliest years, she may have been seen on the Brodess Farm only briefly: when she was scarcely older than a toddler and caring for her younger brother, when she was sent back to her mother after she fell ill while tending muskrat traps near the Little Blackwater River or working on a neighboring farm before she was injured at a store in Bucktown and once again left to her mother's care during her slow recovery.

NEGRO WOMAN FOR SALE.

By virtue of an order of the Orphans' Court of Dorchester County, I will sell, at private sale, a NEGRO WOMAN, slave for life. If not sold by the 7th of October, I will on that day, between the hours of 1 and 3 o'clock, P.M., offer her at public auction, in front of the Court House door, in Cambridge.
Terms: $100 cash, the balance in 6 and 12 months, with notice of approved security.
To be sold to remain in the county.
Isaac M. Neal
Administrator of Micah Neal
Sept. 23, 1857.

(Cambridge) *Democrat*, October 7, 1857

Enslaved people would be sold locally if possible or to "Georgia traders," if necessary, to settle personal debts or estates—a tragedy that tore apart families, such as that of Harriet Tubman.

As you imagine the Brodess Farm in the 1830s and 1840s, scan the farm to search for the other members of Harriet Tubman's family. As was the case with others who had enslaved persons in their households on the border states, where corn and wheat did not require the labor needed for tobacco, cotton, sugar or rice plantations, Edward Brodess inherited more enslaved labor than he needed on his farm. He would have had two choices for raising money with the members of the enslaved Ross family. He either hired out members of the family such as Rit and Minty Ross or sold them south to the cotton lands to a "Georgia trader" coming through the area, as tragically happened to Harriet's sisters Linah, Mariah and Soph.

NEGROES WANTED.

I wish to inform the slave-holders of Dorchester and the adjacent counties that I am again in the market. Persons having negroes that are slaves for life to dispose of will find it to their interest to see me before they sell, as I am determined to pay the highest prices in cash that the southern market will justify. I can be found at A Hall's Hotel in Easton, where I will remain until the first day of July next. Communications addressed to me in Easton, or information given to Wm. Bell, in Cambridge, will meet with prompt attention.

I will be at John Bradshaw's Hotel, in Cambridge, every Monday.
Oct. 6, 1852. Wm. Harker

(Cambridge) *Democrat*, October 27, 1852

An advertisement placed a Cambridge newspaper by a "Georgia Trader."

Don't bother to look for Minty's father, Ben Ross, since he continued to live nearly fifteen miles away (via current roads) from his wife, Rit. The silences you hear at the Brodess Farm may reflect the missing members of the broken family of Ben and Rit Ross and their nine children—sold south or separated across Dorchester at any given time—in vivid and tragic contrast to the daily comings and goings of the eight Brodess children and their parents.

As we read these images, smells and sounds into the scenes of the Brodess Farm, we can appreciate the idea that the landscapes of Harriet Tubman's native land are "virtually unaltered for more than a century." Remembering that virtual can mean "being in essence, not in fact; not actual, but equivalent," we realize the importance of seeing this farm and other Dorchester landscapes known to Harriet Tubman as a *virtual*, not actual, experience of our imagination. In using our imagination to come to grips with the essence of Harriet Tubman's world, we can gain some small measure of her life—its hardships and often its loneliness.

But there is more to Harriet Tubman's virtual landscape than this farm. That broader landscape includes the place of her birth, the locations of her childhood occupations when she was hired out to other families, the place where she received an injury that disabled her for life and the places miles away from this lonely farm where she would work with her father and brothers and where she would make a home with her husband.

Our reading of the landscape of Harriet Tubman's native land must take us once again several miles across Dorchester County and down roads that once had the imprint of her steps.

BRICE STUMP

I was a farm boy who grew up between Bucktown and Cokeland. I had a personal connection with the families here, so I knew their stories. And those stories were tightly woven with each other—one story always led to another. Writing about the legends of Greenbrier Swamp led me to the story of Harriet Tubman. I had learned a little about her in high school, even though she was not part of the school curriculum.

Charlie Ewers.

Old-timers told me that in 1900 this farm of Mr. and Mrs. William Malkus once had a house behind it where two Brodess brothers had lived. It was this Brodess farm where Harriet Tubman had lived and worked, but many of my neighbors had never heard of a "Harriet Tubman." I wrote two articles about her, surprised that no one in our area had previously paid tribute to this woman or the fact that history was made here.

Later I learned from Ms. Mary Pinkett that there was a picture of Harriet Tubman hanging in Bazel's Chapel. Visiting the church, we found the portrait was no longer on the wall but stored away with a Bible in the pulpit: the legend proved true.

Later I received a call from the *Daily Banner* newspaper asking me to go to the unveiling of a new historical plaque at the Brodess farm site. People had read my article and made it happen. I posed for a photo with the other residents of Dorchester County who had in their own ways brought the name of Harriet Tubman back to Bucktown. Harriet Tubman was local. The distance of over one hundred years does not change the fact that this landscape was hers. The Bucktown

store testifies to that landscape being tangible to us today. People who come here can make a connection with that landscape.

Being here makes her story believable. It gives you a taste of what she experienced. You feel the heat or cold or rain as she felt it here when she was at work. It matters to stand here, where she once passed by. It brings her story alive.

Here, between the Greenbrier Swamp and the woods, she lived in a place that was different from the rest of the country and even from neighboring counties on the Shore. It was here in this special place where she stepped onto the stage of history.

—BRICE STUMP

Journalist and author, It Happened in Dorchester, *1969*

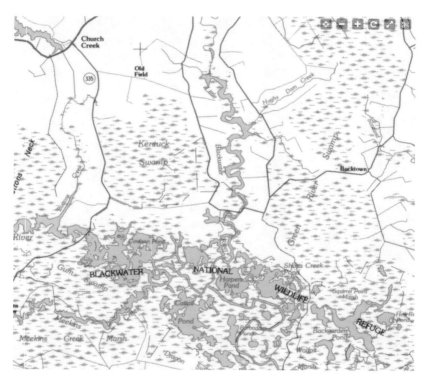

U.S. Soil Conservation Service, Dorchester County, Maryland, 1979. This contemporary map gives us an overview of "Egypt," Harriet Tubman's native land, showing rivers, creeks, marshes, roads and communities. It reveals less about the hidden paths and waterways used by enslaved people to get about and to escape to freedom. According to Samuel Hopkins Adams (*Grandfather Stories*, 1947), Harriet Tubman remained "close-lipped, as a deeply ingrained reticence about secrets that had once meant the difference between slavery and freedom, or even between life or death, for herself and others." By reading the landscape of her native land, we can seek to uncover some of those secrets. *Library of Congress, Geography and Map Division.*

2

The Land of Egypt

CROSSING THE LANDSCAPE OF HARRIET TUBMAN'S NATIVE LAND

"How did you know how to bring them out?"
"The good Lawd was my guide. He fotch us thoo. Besides, I tote a map."
"You couldn't read a map, Aunt Harriet."
"I tote it in my head."
According to the testimony of unimpeachable witnesses, Old Harriet had possessed a miraculous geographical instinct, never forgetting any detail of a route she had once traversed. Thus she was able to pilot unerringly her little, scared bands along unfrequented paths, lying up the day in swamp, cave, or abandoned shack, and dodging the patrols by night.

—Samuel Hopkins Adams, *Grandfather Stories*, 1947

❧

Once when she came to New York, where she had not been in twenty years, and was starting off alone to find some friends miles away in a part of the city which she had never seen, we remonstrated with her, telling her that she surely would be lost. "Now Missus," she said, "don't you t'ink dis ole head dat done the navigatin' down in Egypt can do de navigatin' up here in New York?"

—Sarah Hopkins Bradford, *Harriet, the Moses of Her People*, 1901 edition

Although Harriet Tubman may have used such things as the North Star and the northeast course of rivers on the Eastern Shore, her "navigating," according to Samuel Hopkins Adams, depended most on "never forgetting any detail of a route she had once traversed." As she noted to Sarah Hopkins Bradford, this talent was developed in "Egypt," the land of her enslavement. She would have mastered these skills in Dorchester County along the axis connecting Bucktown with Stewart's Canal and encompassing the places she called home near the Brodess Farm and Peter's Neck. Once we view with our imagination a single place such as the Brodess Farm, we must make use of our mind's eye to navigate as she did across her native land.

Turning away from both the Brodess Farm and Bucktown to the east, take that mind's eye on a trip through the rest of Harriet Tubman's native land by continuing left from the Brodess Farm Site on Greenbrier Road and entering into a wooded area, a stretch of almost one and a half miles leading to Maple Dam Road. This intersection would have been well known to Harriet Tubman in her native land. To the south, it reached the community of Keene's Ditch, where the road ended at the ditch or canal at the edge of the Great Marsh, which connected the high ground of farms and timber to the Blackwater River. To the north, the road led to Cambridge, passing by an African American community that would form the Hughes Mission Methodist Episcopal Church by the time of the Simon Martenet map of Dorchester County of 1866.

Continue your imaginary journey three-eighths of a mile to turn right on an east–west road, the former "Old Mill Road" that would come to be known as Key Wallace Road, named for one of the early managers of the Blackwater National Wildlife Refuge, which was established to the south of the road in 1933. Pass along a neck of land on your left extending into the Great Marsh that would have supported farms on the east side of the Little Blackwater River. A short bridge across the meandering Little Blackwater would have taken you through a ribbon of marsh enclosing the meanders. Harriet Tubman would have known this area through its many family and personal associations. Her mother grew up in the household of Mary Pattison before her marriage to Joseph Brodess (father of Edward). Later, Harriet Tubman would have been hired out in this area, trapping muskrats in a stretch of this marsh.

Now imagine a landscape that Harriet Tubman and her mother would have recognized along the Little Blackwater River we see today. Focus on the trace of a muddy road perhaps marked by ditch banks through a broad

ABOVE: The Key Wallace Trail at Blackwater National Refuge opens into Kentuck Forest, where loggers' skid roads are still visible. These skid roads and other paths may have offered several ways to reach Church Creek, Madison and African American settlements on Peter's Neck and Oldfield. *Charlie Ewers.*

LEFT: *Harriet Tubman Underground Railroad Byway Driving Tour Map, Site 15.*

swath of marsh. We now cross that section beyond the bridge on a modern causeway, since open water covers almost all of the old marsh around the once-meandering river. What was originally the juncture of the Blackwater with the Little Blackwater is a vast bay that is now part of what is called "Lake Blackwater," where the Blackwater similarly once stayed within its own banks with meanders of its own. A side trip on Wildlife Drive in the refuge reveals that this lake today is held back from the refuge only by reinforcement of the shoreline along the drive—where rising waters, sinking land and the erosion that results have radically changed the landscape. The old homestead of Rit Ross and workplace of Harriet Tubman is not only not there but also possibly underwater.

Beyond the causeway west of the Little Blackwater Bridge, Key Wallace Road reaches higher ground that fronts the refuge to the south of the road and still continues to support fields, now cultivated to feed the migratory birds that pass through the marsh in the spring and fall. To the north of the road are stands of loblolly pines that recall the woodlands of Kentuck Forest, bounded to the east by one of several routes to Cambridge, Egypt Road, which perhaps received its name from African Americans living in Cambridge who saw the woodlots and farms worked by enslaved persons to the south in this part of the county as the place "where Israel was in

OPPOSITE: To Harriet Tubman, navigation across Dorchester and Caroline Counties would have meant mastering a network of thoroughfares—including paths, roads, stream crossings, landings for skiffs and footbridges such as this. *Charlie Ewers.*

ABOVE: In the day of Harriet Tubman, this road would have been a muddy track that made a beeline from the bridge across the snaking Little Blackwater River to the higher ground at the entrance to today's Wildlife Drive at the Blackwater National Wildlife Refuge. It is now an elevated causeway through "Lake Blackwater," the swollen course of the Blackwater River that once also meandered in a narrow passage through the current refuge. *Charlie Ewers.*

Egypt land" as described in the spiritual "Go Down Moses." This was the geographical center of the land that shaped the life of the young Minty Ross, who would become the Underground Railroad conductor known as "Moses," in her early life in Dorchester.

Two miles beyond the intersection with Egypt Road, Key Wallace Road meets the present-day Maryland Highway 335. A left turn south on this road today will take you to the Harriet Tubman Underground Railroad Visitor Center. Imagine a road and paths there in Harriet Tubman's time that could have taken her west across Button's (Barton's) Creek through the woods to Peter's Neck, the location of her old home. Or turn left and go another fraction of a mile to the current Blackwater bridge, where in the day you might see Harriet Tubman making her way upriver to the old homeplace. Either way, think of her taking a skiff, whether to cross Button's Creek or to row up the Blackwater.

To continue your imaginary exploration of Harriet Tubman's Dorchester world, turn right at the intersection of Key Wallace Road and Highway 335 and go four miles north toward the town of Church Creek. With your mind's eye, you can imagine a string of farms on the left hemmed in by Buttons Creek and on the right a few fronting Kentuck Forest. One mile south of Church Creek you will pass the road to Oldfield, an African American community of farmers and woodchoppers, centered on the Vaughn ME Church and Beverly School, named for the "old field" or loblolly pines that grew where forests had been cleared or fields abandoned.

At Church Creek, turn left on Maryland Highway 16 and follow Harriet Tubman's footsteps just over eight miles west to Madison (once known as Tobacco Stick), where her work with her father for the Stewart family's timber and shipbuilding enterprises would have been focused. Use your imagination to project back in time to a somewhat different landscape from the docks for workboats and pleasure craft currently found in Madison. Think back to the boatyard, the sawpits or perhaps a steam sawmill, where boat timbers would be shaped and fitted together. Find the dock, where passengers would depart for Baltimore by steamboat.

PREVIOUS: Once a marsh surrounding a curving Little Blackwater River where it met the Blackwater, this scene is now part of the so-called Lake Blackwater. *Charlie Ewers.*

OPPOSITE: At the very least, the trails in Harriet Tubman's native land would have been muddy. Sometimes they required deep wading or balancing to cross a footbridge. *Charlie Ewers.*

ABOVE: Oldfield was graced by Vaughn Methodist Episcopal Church decades after Harriet Tubman left her native land but may have been an African American settlement that existed in her time. *Charlie Ewers.*

OPPOSITE: A loblolly (oldfield) pine springing up in cleared timberlands near the community of Oldfield. *Charlie Ewers.*

Perhaps nestled in the fields just beyond the waterside, you can see a grove of trees nearby, where congregants white and Black would attend the annual Tobacco Stick Camp Meeting—some even taking charter steamboats from Baltimore.

Follow Harriet Tubman's footsteps by turning south from Madison on what is now called White Marsh Road and proceeding one mile to reach the edge of the Peter's Neck community, more recently known as Outback and marked by the more recent Malone's (or Malon's) Chapel and the larger fields of corn, milo or soybeans grown in Dorchester today. Scan up and down the road to imagine the time when small farms were clustered along this road—some of which were worked by enslaved persons, some of which belonged to free African Americans. Imagine the small slave quarters where Harriet Tubman was born and—likely not far away—the cabin she would have shared with her free husband, John Tubman.

From Madison, let your imagination take you another two and a half miles to the west on Highway 16 to where it crosses Stewart's Canal. Think back to skiffs filled with cordwood being poled or small log rafts being tracked by someone walking along the bank to the narrow island south of today's road, where the wood and timber could be unloaded on either side to be transported by boat to Madison. Look back to the time when a narrow band of marsh separated the canal from the woods the canal was dug to harvest. The current marsh and surrounding ghost forests of dead trees created by the washing of flooding tides in and out between Parson's Creek on the Little Choptank to the north and the upper Blackwater River flowing into Fishing Bay to the south would barely be recognizable to Harriet Tubman today.

Not counting errands in Cambridge and work with her father and brothers in places such as Poplar Neck on the Dorchester border with Caroline County, Harriet Tubman's life in her native land of Dorchester would have coursed along the stretch you have imagined, an axis of twenty

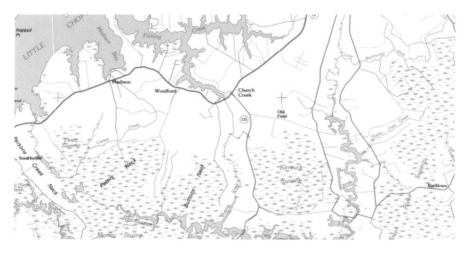

TOP: This detail of the Soil Conservation Service Map of Dorchester County, Maryland, 1979, shows the communities north of Bucktown and the Blackwater River, including Madison, Stewart's Canal and Peter's Neck, where Harriet Tubman was born and where she worked just before she left "Egypt" for freedom. *Library of Congress, Geography and Map Division.*

BOTTOM: The calm of modern-day Madison (formerly Tobacco Stick) would have been a contrast with the activity of this shipbuilding center and steamboat dock in Harriet Tubman's time. With a bit of imagination, the visitor today might hear the sawing of timber, hammering together of boats, chugging of the steamboat coming to its dockage offshore and screeching of a boat whistle for lighters to approach the steamer to offload passengers and cargo. *Charlie Ewers.*

to twenty-one miles. The paths and side roads that may have provided shortcuts to Harriet Tubman might have reduced the mileage but would have posed their own challenges with mud wallows and creek crossings that would have required wading, balancing on a flimsy bridge or rowing a skiff. However, even the main roads would have been nearly impassable at times—challenging the walker, rider, drover or wagoner with drifting snow in winter, pools of rain or tide water in summer and deep mire all of the year. Think about covering that near-marathon distance in the best of conditions with dry roads and good weather. Dare to imagine going even a fraction of the distance down muddy roads or through high snowdrifts or during a summer gale or winter storm.

Now exercise your imagination even further by going seven times the distance you have taken today, following the Underground Railroad from Harriet Tubman's native land to Philadelphia, a distance of 150 miles. Prepare in your mind starting your journey—alone or later with others—skirting the town of Church Creek and the southern edge of Cambridge before heading south and then east toward Delaware. Think about how you would take that long and dangerous journey for the first time through the countryside, armed only perhaps with the knowledge of the rivers pointing northeast and acquaintance with or hearsay of a sympathetic Black or white "stationmaster." Although like the other rivers of the Eastern Shore it pointed toward freedom, the Choptank River that served as the northern boundary of Dorchester County would have been a barrier for most of its length—give or take an exposed ferry crossing or two—until it reached into Caroline County, forcing you (as the river impelled Harriet Tubman) to take any number of routes via East New Market toward Delaware and the arteries that went northward toward Wilmington, Delaware, to cross the line to freedom just south of Philadelphia, Pennsylvania.

Now consider a few options that would have aided "Moses" on her travels. In the last few years of Harriet Tubman's rescue missions into Dorchester, she would have had recourse to the north–south Delaware Railroad, which made its way to Seaford on the Nanticoke River by the late 1850s. At various times in the 1850s, she would have had steamboats that connected the county as well along the rivers that otherwise served as barriers to the Underground Railroad. The *Champion* ran round trips once a week from Baltimore to Taylor's Island, Tobacco Stick and Church Creek and to Cambridge, Easton (in Talbot County) and Denton (in Caroline County). The *Hugh Jenkins* ran to Deal's Island (in Somerset County), Hooper's Straits (near Crapo), Vienna and Seaford, Delaware. Accompany Harriet Tubman making use of these

OPPOSITE, TOP: Stewart's Canal provided access to the timberlands out of reach of the Blackwater River, bringing in logs and cordwood by raft or barge to larger boats in Parson's Creek on the Little Choptank River. *Charlie Ewers.*

OPPOSITE, BOTTOM: Corsey Creek, rerouted and deepened to serve as a canal, joined Stewart's Canal to Madison sometime between 1847 and 1877, opening up additional timberlands to the south and east of Madison Bay. Both parts of today's U-shaped waterway eventually washed into the headwaters of the Blackwater River, creating the tidal flows between the Little Choptank River and Fishing Bay that would overwhelm the freshwater marshes and create the ghost forests along the upper reaches of the Blackwater. *Charlie Ewers.*

ABOVE: The waters and land near Poplar Neck in Caroline County, where Harriet Tubman first attempted to depart for the north. *Charlie Ewers.*

FOLLOWING: "Ursa Major directed the poor fugitives in America in former days to the pole star, that, as they followed, led them to a land of freedom." Joseph J. Neave, "Letter to the Editor." "The pole-star guiding the slave to liberty" was a reference that dated several decades before this reference. *From* The British Friend, *March 15, 1881; Charlie Ewers.*

routes and the Chesapeake and Delaware Canal, knowing that you could be apprehended at any time in an enclosed boat cabin or railroad car despite your forged permit letters purporting to be from a slaveowner or employer.

If you have gone far afield using your imagination to peer into the past of these places near and far, you will have become a thorough landscape reader visiting these sites or following the Harriet Tubman Underground Railroad Byway. Channeling your imagination through your senses, you will be able to carry yourself back in time to Harriet Tubman's native land. If the sights, sounds and smells disagree with you, try to accept them for what they are: signs of a rough life and livelihood made worse by the brutality, privation, poverty, anxiety and suffering as an enslaved person. But also don't forget that these conditions forged strong families and heroism in big and small ways, as they did in the early life of Harriet Tubman.

Now refuel your imagination in reading the landscape through the exhibits of the Harriet Tubman Underground Railroad Visitor Center, the centerpiece of the axis of landscapes of Harriet Tubman's native land. Explore the exhibits, complete the interactive exercises (such as the *Junior Ranger Activity Book*) and walk the paths around the Legacy Garden. If you can channel yourself back in time during your walk, perhaps you will catch a glimpse of Minty Ross or hear her steps or even her singing a heartfelt song as she makes her way from Peter's Neck to the edge of Greenbrier Swamp.

Finally, once you have made use of your mind's eye to imagine the landscape of the Brodess Farm (or any other location in Harriet Tubman's native land), do not forget to refocus your eyes, other senses and, most of all, your heart into the present. Accept that the backdrop of nature has changed with the harvesting of timber and flooding of marshes. Acknowledge that the human landscape has changed in scale, technology, livelihood and, especially, the laws that govern rights and relationships.

But never forget that a profound courage once shaped the human dimensions in the location of this farm and resounds to us nearly two centuries after the formative years of a young woman and the lives of

OPPOSITE, TOP: Harriet Tubman Underground Railroad Visitor Center offers a variety of resources to help you focus your mind's eye on the Dorchester landscape of the past. *Charlie Ewers.*

OPPOSITE, BOTTOM: When you visit the Brodess Farm Site, treat it with respect—not only for the current owners of the property but also for what happened here in Harriet Tubman's day. That story and its setting can be seen in your mind's eye by reading the landscape and immersing yourself in the history that shaped it. *Charlie Ewers.*

the people she knew in her native land. That young woman mastered this seemingly intimidating landscape—slipping through fences, bypassing roads and leading people to freedom from its confines.

That courage lends a sacredness to this land that goes beyond today's industrial farm fields, dying trees, flooded marshes and fallen houses. We should not hesitate to cherish what we may not see now, but feel. As Harriet Tubman biographer Kate Clifford Larson observed about the current Bucktown General Store, rebuilt or renovated in the 1860s, "We should accord the site and view the building and what it represents with respect."

As you read this book and pass through all of these sites known and unknown, unlock your imagination to draw your re-created landscapes of Harriet Tubman's native land, but never forget to respect them, as you might honor the Brodess Farm with its uniform crop of soybeans or corn and a tumbledown house as a sacred place too for what it means to us today. As we have seen, the old home is long gone, but there is much of value to us that remains where it once stood.

ANGELA CRENSHAW

When people of all ages come to the Harriet Tubman Underground Railroad Visitor Center, they discover what speaks uniquely to them. Afterward, they may visit the Bucktown Store to see where Tubman was injured and nearly killed by a two-pound weight. They may drive along Wildlife Drive at the Blackwater National Wildlife Refuge to see the river where she worked. They may cross the Little Blackwater River to see where she trapped muskrats as a child.

Charlie Ewers.

We learn so much from questions posed by visitors to Maryland park rangers at Harriet Tubman Underground Railroad Visitor Center, including what has meaning to the people who come here. Often women will ask if Harriet Tubman was married. They learn about her marriage to John Tubman and then may visit Malone's Chapel (Malone's Methodist Episcopal Church), located where there was a thriving community of free and enslaved African Americans during Tubman's time in Dorchester County. They also discover that John Tubman remarried after Harriet Tubman's self-emancipation and had no desire to be with her when she returned to see him.

We learn what speaks to young people through the *Junior Ranger Activity Book* created by Maryland park rangers at the Visitor Center. Guests of all ages answer quantitative and qualitative questions listed in the book, discovering the answers by studying the book or through exploring the exhibits in the Visitor Center. They answer questions such as "what does freedom mean to you?" They find numbers connected to Harriet Tubman's life, such as the year she was born. When they complete the questions, they take the Junior Ranger

Pledge and receive a Junior Ranger Patch. But they get so much more in return. They build a personal connection to Harriet Tubman and her network of supporters on the Underground Railroad.

They begin their preparation to become a Junior Ranger by writing their own name and drawing their picture. If you don't know yourself, you cannot hope to understand Harriet Tubman. Near the end of their preparation, they explain how they received their names—one of the most popular assignments. One time a young woman asked her mother how she received her first and middle names. Her mother told her that her first name was from her mother's favorite aunt—now deceased—and her middle name was from her mother's grandmother—also deceased. In telling her daughter this, the mother teared up and so did her daughter—we all did as well.

I believe that guests who visit the outdoor picnic pavilion also will feel their time here speak to them. Guests cook for the family, help each other with the preparations and have fellowship around a meal. They slow down and enjoy quality time together at a state park dedicated to an important and often misunderstood American heroine. Harriet Tubman's life story of faith and family echoes throughout the day for them.

As someone who loves the outdoors, I love to walk on the trails at the Visitor Center. They speak to me. I look for the deer tracks and scat. I watch the flight of the butterflies. I gaze up and see a bald eagle saluting me with a dip of his wing. Nature truly shows off here.

Along the trails, I also think about this place—less than five miles as the crow flies from where she was born and less than ten miles from the Bucktown Village Store. This landscape is where Tubman began her journey to freedom along the south–north axis illustrated by the floorplan of the Visitor Center. I think about her learning the skills she would use on the way north. I think of her traveling at night on the Underground Railroad—sometimes alone at night and feeling the cold bitter wind that blows across the flat lands of Dorchester County in the winter.

When we connect with the landscape here, I think that all of us— visitors and staff, young people and adults—have an "aha" moment about Harriet Tubman's life and legacy. That realization brings the hand to the chest and takes the story full circle to the heart.

—RANGER ANGELA CRENSHAW
Area Manager, Gunpowder Falls State Park
Former Assistant Manager, Harriet Tubman Underground Railroad State Park

3

A Neglected Weed

STARTING LIFE IN THE SLAVE QUARTERS

"An' so you wants to hear de story ob Harriet's life all over agin,"
she said. "Pairs like youse heard it so many times you could
tell dat story you self."

—as told to Emma Paddock Telford, *Harriet: The Modern Moses of Heroism and Visions*, circa 1905. Courtesy Cayuga Museum of History and Art.

"Well, in eastern shore of Maryland Dorchester County
is where I was borned."

—Emma Paddock Telford, *Harriet: The Modern Moses of Heroism and Visions*, circa 1905

This bridge across the upper Blackwater River is a crossing that a century ago connected Harrisville Road leading north to Madison with roads and paths that went south to Golden Hill. Beyond the marsh and thinning stand of trees in the background are the farms of Peter's Neck, the center of much of Harriet Tubman's Dorchester life. In contrast with the large oak trees that grew in this area in Harriet Tubman's time, ghost forests of dying loblolly pines today give way to marsh—itself being flooded by the widening river. *Charlie Ewers.*

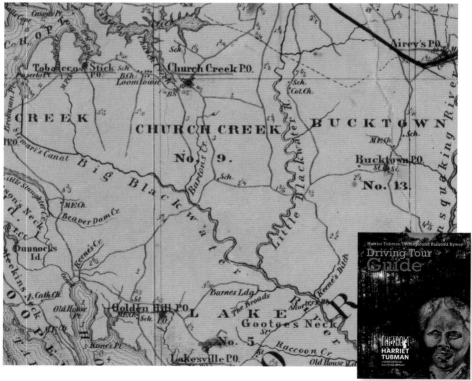

[A] thin line of frame houses...where farm laborers and boat helpers live....Farms and woodlots are the main features of the landscape....Farther down the Whitemarsh Road, which was called Peter's Neck Road 50 years ago, there is a marshy section.

—John C. Schmidt, "Out Back—Where and Why," (Baltimore) *Sun*, May 21, 1960

She was born, she said, in the eastern part of the state of Maryland, and wanted it to be distinctly understood that she was not educated, nor did she receive any "broughtin up"; she "came up."

—*Brooklyn Daily Eagle*, "Mrs. Harriet Tubman, the Colored Nurse and Scout—The Bridge Street African M.E. Church Last Evening," October 23, 1865

OPPOSITE, TOP: Passing the community known as Outback, White Marsh Road led to the upper Blackwater River, helping to delineate Peter's Neck along with the parallel Harrisville Road to the east. This quiet stretch of road, anchored by the now-closed Malone's Church, contrasts with the lively community of the nineteenth and early twentieth centuries, when wood-chopping and farming employed African Americans who lived down the road. *Charlie Ewers*.

OPPOSITE, BOTTOM: Simon J. Martenet, "Dorchester County," 1866. The northwest quadrant of this map shows how the Peter's Neck roads connected the timberlands along the Blackwater with the mills and wharves of the Little Choptank River. It also shows Stewart's Canal, a more efficient alternative to bringing out timber along the roads with steers, as was done on Harrisville Road, once called Thompson's New Road for the man who built it for hauling logs, Anthony Thompson, who had custody of the young Edward Brodess and the enslaved people who were conveyed to him—including Rit Ross and her daughter Harriet Ross Tubman—upon the death of Thompson's wife, Mary Pettison Brodess Thompson. *From Martenet's Atlas of Maryland, 1865*.

INSET: *Harriet Tubman Underground Railroad Byway Driving Tour Map, Site 8.*

"RIDGETON FARMS" RESIDENCE AND GROUNDS OF JUDGE LEVI D. TRAVERS TAYLOR'S ISLAND DORCHESTER CO. MD.

HARRIET TUBMAN was born in Dorchester County, Maryland, about the year 1820 *[sic, actually 1822]*. She was held as a slave, although there is reason to believe that but for a fraudulent transaction she and her mother would have been free according to the provisions of a former master's will. Harriet was one of ten *[sic, actually nine]* children. While she was very little, two *[sic]* of her older sisters were sold, chained up with other negroes and driven away. She perched on the top of a fence and watched them go, crying as they went.

—Lillie B. Chace Wyman, "Harriet Tubman," *New England Magazine*, March 1896

ABOVE: This idealized picture of Ridgeton Farms, "Residence and Grounds of Judge Levi Travers, Taylor's Island, Dorchester Co., Md.," in Lake, Griffing & Stevenson, relegate the quarters of the farmhands to the background of the scene. The modern photo of this site may challenge us to look within this landscape for stories such as that of Harriet Tubman. *From* Illustrated Atlas of Talbot & Dorchester Counties, Maryland, *1877.*

OPPOSITE, TOP: The "Big House" of Ridgeton Farms is still there, but not the "Little Houses" seen in Lake, Griffing & Stevenson. *From* Illustrated Atlas of Talbot & Dorchester Counties, Maryland, *1877.*

OPPOSITE, BOTTOM: This spot near the meeting point of Stewart's and Corsey Creek canals was probably forested on both sides of the water. It is a likely place where Harriet Tubman would have gathered roots and herbs as a child and taken timber for her father as an adult. The timber is long gone on the north bank and thinning out on the south, victim of the salty water from Parson's Creek. *Charlie Ewers.*

"Mammy and Pappy and me lived in a house close to the big house back there....The big house was two stories high with a big porch what run clean to the top, and more window blinds that I ever seen in a house since. Our little house was made of planks, heavy oak lumber all whitewashed with lime."

—Ethel Wolfe Garrison, "Interview with Henry Clay Ex-Slave," 1937

Araminta Ross, now known by her married name of Tubman, with her sounding Christian name changed to Harriet, is the granddaughter of a slave imported from Africa, and has not a drop of white blood in her veins.

—Franklin B. Sanborn, "Harriet Tubman," (Boston) *Commonwealth*, 1863

Her parents were Benjamin Ross and Harriet Green, both slaves, but married to each other. She had ten brothers and sisters, three of whom she rescued from slavery during the Civil War. She also rescued her father and mother through the "underground railway."

—*Auburn Daily Advertiser*, "Death of Aunt Harriet, 'Moses of her People,'" March 11, 1913

The old mammies...were wont to nod knowingly and say, "I reckon youse one o' dem 'Shantees,' chile." For they knew the tradition of the unconquerable Ashantee blood, which in a slave made him a thorn in the side of the planter.

—Frank C. Drake, "The Moses of Her People," *New York Herald*, September 22, 1907

"I grew, up like a neglected weed—ignorant of liberty, having no experience of it. Then I was not happy or contented."

—Harriet Tubman, in Benjamin Drew, *A North-Side View of Slavery*, 1856

African American slave families owned by Mrs. Barnwell, circa 1860–65. An enslaved family could consist of nine children, as was the case with Harriet Tubman. *Library of Congress.*

The cabins or huts of the slaves were small, and were built principally by the slaves themselves, as they could find time on Sundays and moonlight nights; they went into the swamps, cut the logs, hacked or hauled them to the quarters and put up their cabins.

—*Narrative of Nehemiah Caulkins*, 1849

We dwelt in log cabins, and on the bare ground. Wooden floors were an unknown luxury to the slave.

—*Autobiography of James L. Smith*, 1881

Labor in the mills of the early days was of course done by slaves for whom the planters (owners) built specially designed houses called "quarters."…[T]he ventilation of their "quarters" with large open fire-places sufficient to hold large sticks of wood accounted for their general good health.

—James S. Shepherd, "Watermills and Windmills of Dorchester County," (Dorchester) *Daily Banner*, March 10, 1934

Making several generalizations without evidence or personal experience, the author suggests that a smoky, drafty slave quarters would have "accounted for" the "general good health" of enslaved people.

"*[D]*e man took me up front ob him on de hoss an' off we went....I was like de boy on de Suwanes Ribber, 'no place I lake my ole cabin home.' Whenever you saw a chile wasser homesick dan I wuz, you see a bad one....

I useter tink all de time ef I could only git home an' git in my muder's bed, an' de funny part of dat was, she nebber had a bade in her life. Nuffin but a board box nailed up agin de wall an' straw laid on it. I stayed dere two years."

—Emma Paddock Telford, *Harriet: The Modern Moses of Heroism and Visions*, circa 1905

ABOVE: Slave quarters, Cambridge, Maryland. The "little houses" of a farm could also be built behind the "big houses" of a town for household servants. This one may have housed enslaved and/ or free families working for a family living in the county seat of Dorchester County. *Charlie Ewers.*

There were neither furniture nor bedsteads of any description; our beds were collections of straw and old rags, thrown down in the corners; some were boxed in with boards, while others were old ticks filled with straw. All ideas of decency and refinement were, of course, out of the question....

At night, each slept rolled up in a coarse blanket; one partition, which was an old quilt or blanket, or something else that answered the purpose, was extended across the hut; wood partitions were unknown to the doomed slave.

—*Autobiography of James L. Smith*, 1881

"De fust ting I member, was lyin' in de cradle. Youse seen dese trees dat ar hollow. Take a big tree, cut it down, put a bode in each and, make a cradle of it and call it a 'gum.'"

—Emma Paddock Telford, *Harriet: The Modern Moses of Heroism and Visions*, circa 1905

To make a cradle to rock the baby in, we took a hollow buckeye and split the log, and put rockers on the bottom.

—E. Tucker, "W.M. Botkin (1816)," *History of Randolph County, Indiana*, 1882

OPPOSITE, TOP: A "gum" was any kind of box-like container, usually made from the wood of the red gum tree that grew in swampy areas, including the "diving gums," wooden traps that Harriet Tubman may have used to catch muskrats. *Charlie Ewers*.

OPPOSITE, BOTTOM: This gum made to be a baby's cradle was carved by Warren Saunders and Ron Tatman from a Dorchester County tree for Harriet Tubman Underground Railroad State Park. *Charlie Ewers*.

The provision for each slave, per week, was a peck of corn, two dozens of herrings, and about four pounds of meat. The children, under eight years of age, were not allowed anything.

—*Life of John Thompson, a Fugitive Slave*, 1856

A water pail, a boiling pot, and a few gourds made up the furniture. When the corn had been ground in a hand-mill, and then boiled, the pot was swung from the fire and the children squatted around it, with oyster shells for spoons. Sweet potatoes, oysters and crabs varied the diet....

The allowance for the slave men for the week was a peck-and-a-half of corn meal, and two pounds of bacon. The women's allowance was a peck of meal and from one pound-and-a-half to two pounds of bacon; and so much for each child, varying from one half to a peck a week, and of bacon, from one-half to a pound a week. In order to make our allowance hold out, we went crabbing or fishing. In the winter season we used to go hunting nights, catching oysters, coons and possums.

—*Autobiography of James L. Smith*, 1881

"De man come after me ridin' hossback. I hadn't any clos', but I was anxious to go, an' de mistis made me a petticoat."

—Emma Paddock Telford, *Harriet: The Modern Moses of Heroism and Visions*, circa 1905

The slaves' clothing was, in winter, one shirt, pants and jacket, without lining, shoes and stockings. In summer, one shirt and one pair of pants of coarse linen.

—*Life of John Thompson, a Fugitive Slave*, 1856

PLANTERS SAVE YOUR MONEY

All that are in want of good Negro and House servant's shoes would do well to call the NEW SHOE STORE of Workman & Boone, and examine their stock before purchasing elsewhere.

Good wages will be paid for six or eight good workmen.

Workman & Boone

(Camden, South Carolina) *Weekly Journal*, October 31, 1849

Slavery gave rise to a specialized product line of "Negro shoes."

Our dress was made of tow cloth; for the children, nothing was furnished them but a shirt; for the older ones, a pair of pantaloons or a gown, in addition, according to the sex. Besides these, in the winter season an overcoat, or a round jacket; a wool hat once in two or three years for the men, and a pair of coarse brogan shoes once a year.

—*Autobiography of James L. Smith*, 1881

"*[W]*hen I wuz fo' or five years ole, my mother cooked up to the big house and' lef me to take care ob de baby an' my little brudder."

"I use ter be in a hurry fer *[my mother]* to go, so's I could play de baby was a pig in a bag, an' hole him up by de bottom ob his dress. I had a nice frolic wid dat baby, swingin' him all 'roun, his feet in de dress an' his little head an arms techin de flo', cause Ise too small to hold him higher."

—Emma Paddock Telford, *Harriet: The Modern Moses of Heroism and Visions,* circa 1905

[T]he first work he remembered doing was "nussing a baby boy of Mr. Bramwell Burden, a gran'son of old man Burden."

—Nelson Birdsong, Mobile, Alabama, Federal Writers' Project, Slave Narrative Project, Vol. 1, Alabama, 1936–37

"It was late nights fore my mother's git home, an' when hed get worryin' I'd cut a fat chunk ob pork an' toast it on de coals an' put it in his mouf. One night he went to sleep wid dat hangin' out, an' my mother came home she thought I'd done kill him."

—Emma Paddock Telford, *Harriet: The Modern Moses of Heroism and Visions*, circa 1905

ABOVE: Russell Lee, "Children of Negro Family Living on Strawberry Farm," 1939. As in the early life of Harriet Tubman, children cared for other children while their parents and older siblings worked during the day. *Library of Congress.*

DORNELL WOOLFORD

Harriet Tubman had mother-wit, a gift from God. It was in the form of communication, leadership and caring for others. Why did she have that ability? What craft makes a carpenter or boat builder without formal knowledge of math? What instinct makes a nurse without training? I believe mother-wit is an instinctual function, an innate ability that is divine in origin.

Harriet Tubman likely received some of her mother-wit from her mother, especially her abilities to nurse, but she also received some "father-wit," learning from Ben Ross a sense of topography and how to find her way to and from the backwoods of Dorchester County, such as using the moss growing on trees to find north. She used those talents to travel back and forth. Finding her way back to Dorchester must have been instinctual, innate for her, a journey home.

The mother-wit she used in caring for children as a very young girl she employed with the children she led out of Dorchester County. She used it, too, for nursing soldiers in South Carolina and residents at her home in Auburn, New York. It was the same skill.

Her mother-wit came from God instilling it. It was not witchcraft or any form of sorcery. She used it to do good for others. Her faith was based on a deep knowledge of songs and spirituals. She showed her mother-wit through music, pulling the songs out of her head and having faith that the God she served would deliver her. She had no text to read as she had no formal teaching of music or prose. She would even change the words to the songs as needed. Those songs live on today in us.

She put her spiritual sensitivity to work in sending signals and evading pursuers on the Underground Railroad, but that spirituality also translated into a gift to preach. She knew what to say, how to say it and how to reach people. This skill came in handy in escorting her "passengers" to safety.

When I see the Peter's Neck landscape where Harriet Tubman was born, I remember a similar place near Maple Dam as the happiest place I could ever be. As a child, I remember my father taking us to New Hughes Mission to worship with his mother, cousins and extended family. Although different in color and size, his family church was set at the fork of two roads. No running water. No bathroom. People thankful for God's grace. A wood stove for cold days. My grandmother provided the communion. I would spend some weekends with my grandmother in her house— like the church, without a bathroom. Although she

Charlie Ewers.

didn't have a driver's license, she took a chance a few times by driving us to church in the family car along the backroads near Blackwater Refuge; otherwise, she managed to have relatives transport us to her place of worship. We had to attend church! Her church had no church hall, so for festive occasions we had our supper outside. In that sense, the church was the center of the Black community, a community center of sorts, where people knew that on at least one day a week—"Come Sunday, oh come Sunday," in the words of Duke Ellington, "That's the day"—everything would be alright. Malone's Church and others like it represented healing, not just for the sin-sick soul but healing from the pain and agony of what happened to that group of people outside its church walls. Certainly, I cannot attest to what this church looked like 180 years ago, but today, even with some visual disrepair, worn and tired, it still stands serenely along a narrow road to tell, in part, the early life of Harriet Tubman and many like her.

This church and its grounds are an idyllic place today, quiet, virtually untouched and remote. It stands as direct or indirect witness to the eras of slavery, emancipation, Jim Crow, civil rights and modern technology. To its side is a cemetery, neatly kept and grass mowed. When Harriet Tubman escaped it, this place probably represented a

double-edged sword for her. Perhaps she saw it as a positive place in her life where she and her family worshipped, but she came back to this place where she grew up only to lead people away to freedom. How do you leave a place you love? You leave simply because it hurts you to stay. I suspect the simplicity of the Malone's Church structure and the physical landscape that surround it are not vastly different than the landscape of Tubman's time. I am thankful for its simplicity, its flat land, trees and vines as it stands as a beautiful reminder of the greatness of God's love and of an enslaved people that endured. I hope to never lose a place like this church, for it, hopefully, can continue to teach the generations that follow me that Harriet Tubman lived in this community. When she left it, she nonetheless left behind a legacy which is our freedom.

Fortunately, only the beauty and simplicity of this church remain today. For the sake of good things that happened in this church and as a temporary shield against the bad things that happened to enslaved people that extended from within to just outside its walls, this church remains. I don't want us to lose a place like this. It helps me peel back the layers of the past and marvel at how far we have come: "My soul looks back and wonders how I got over."

—DORNELL L. WOOLFORD, PHD
Weekend and Evening Administrator
Wor-Wic Community College

4

The Sting of the Whip

TRAPPING IN THE MARSH AND
LABORING FOR A MISTRESS

These marshes in Bestpitch once were among the most productive areas in Dorchester County for trapping muskrats. Overwhelmed by sinking lands and ever higher tides, they now are a shadow of the kind of wetlands where Harriet Tubman tended her traps near the meeting of the Blackwater and Little Blackwater Rivers. The young "Minty" Ross, hired under ten years of age, trapped muskrats in winter, suffering the first of several serious illnesses. She was sent back to her mother, who nursed her back to health so that she could be hired out again. *Charlie Ewers.*

"[L]ike de boy on de Swanee Ribber, 'no place lake my ole cabin home.' Whenever you saw a chile wasser homesick dan I waz, you see a bad one."

—Emma Paddock Telford, *Harriet: The Modern Moses of Heroism and Visions*, circa 1905

The lands in the *[southern]* parts of the county are low and marshy; particularly along Transquaking, Blackwater, and *[Farm]* creeks....The principal produce is corn, wheat, and lumber.

—Joseph Scott, *Geographical Description of the States of Maryland and Delaware*, 1807

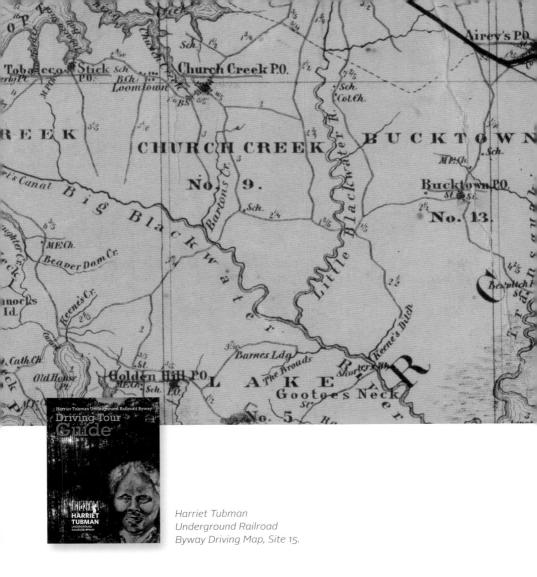

Harriet Tubman
Underground Railroad
Byway Driving Map, Site 15.

ABOVE: Simon J. Martenet, "Dorchester County," 1866. The land east of the Little Blackwater River has supported farms for centuries. *From* Martenet's Atlas of Maryland, *1865.*

OPPOSITE: Heading west from Maple Dam Road on Key Wallace Drive (once known as Old Mill Road, since it led to the mill once located at today's Blackwater Bridge on Highway 335), one sees the high ground that supported farms a few miles away from the Brodess Farm and east of the winding Little Blackwater River. Harriet Tubman worked here for James Cook and his family, first doing household chores to support the women in the house. *Charlie Ewers.*

When Harriet was six years old, she was taken from her mother and carried ten *[sic, more likely two]* miles to live with James Cook, whose wife was a weaver, to learn the trade of weaving....

Another attempt was made to teach her weaving, but she would not learn, for she hated her mistress, and did not want to live at home, as she would have done as a weaver, for it was the custom then to weave the cloth for the family, or a part of it, in the house.

—Franklin B. Sanborn, "Harriet Tubman," (Boston) *Commonwealth*, 1863

ABOVE: "Lucindy Lawrence Jurdon, age 79," *WPA Slave Narrative* (Alabama), 1936–1938, demonstrating her mother's spinning wheel. *Library of Congress.*

*Through the winter and on rainy days in summer, the women...
had to card the wool and spin it into yarn. They generally
worked in pairs, a spinning wheel and cards being assigned to
each pair, and while one carded the wool into rolls, the other
spun it into yarn suitable for weaving into cloth....[T]he women
working together alternated in the carding and spinning....*

*One woman did the weaving and it was her task to weave
from nine to ten yards a day. Aunt Liza was our weaver
and she was taught the work by the madam. At first she did
not get on so well with it and many times I have seen the
madam jump at her, pinch and choke her because she was
dull in understanding how to do it. The madam made the
unreasonable demand that she should do the full task at first,
and because she failed she was punished, as was the custom in
all cases of failure, no matter how unreasonable the demand.
Liza finally became equal to her task and accomplished it
each day.*

—Louis Hughes, *Thirty Years a Slave*, 1897

&

The slaves had to weave cotton and
knit sox. Sometimes they would work
all night, weaving cloth and spinning
thread. The spinning would be done
first. They would make cloth for all
the hands on the place.

—Cyrus Bellus, *WPA Slave Narratives*, Vol. 2, Arkansas, Part 1, 1938

She would go to her loom, and from daylight till dark, with the exception of the dinner-hour, up and down would go the treadles, in and out would fly the shuttles, back and forth would swing the heavy lathe. No steam nor waterpower moved that loom—mother's hands and feet did it all.

I used often to wonder how she could throw the shuttle through so quickly. It would go like a dart—back and forth—from one hand to the other—and as it left either hand she would grasp the lathe, and as quickly as the other hand drew out the shuttle, she would "bang" the thread up into place. That was the work it required for each single thread of the "filling"—to treadle, to throw the shuttle, and to drive up the thread. Not to speak of the spinning, the spooling, the warping, the beaming, and the winding of quills to fill the shuttles, see how much work there was in weaving one yard of cloth.

—M.L.O., "My Mother's Loom," *Arthur's Illustrated Home Magazine*, 1873

One of the treadle looms at Furnace Town Living Heritage Village is around two hundred years old. The other (the larger, lighter-colored one) is closer to three hundred years old and originally came from England to a farm in Stockton, Maryland, according to the man who donated it.

It would probably be too difficult and tedious for a young girl (such as Harriet Tubman) to warp (set up) one of these looms or to actually work the treadles for weaving, but she could be put to work cutting strips of cloth to be used for making rugs, winding the shuttle, or working the beater bar.

—Grace Tartaglia, Furnace Town Historic Site

TOP: Jack Delano, "Mrs. Patrick Dumond, weaving toweling on an old loom in the attic," 1940. *Library of Congress.*

BOTTOM, LEFT: On display in the Furnace Town Historic Site in neighboring Worcester County, these looms—one of which is from the time of Harriet Tubman leaving Dorchester County—strike today's visitor as an intimidating sight. It would have been all the more so for a young child, torn from her family and hired out to learn weaving. *Charlie Ewers.*

BOTTOM, RIGHT: Treadle loom (detail), Furnace Town Historic Site. *Charlie Ewers.*

Don Massa has about a thousand sheep and he gits de wool, and de niggers cards and spins and weaves it, and dat makes all de clothes.

—Andy J. Anderson, *WPA Slave Narratives*, Vol. 16, Texas, Part 1, 1936-38

ABOVE: Grace Tartaglia weaving, Furnace Town Historic Site. *Charlie Ewers.*

OPPOSITE: The "vast prairie" of the Great Marsh in Dorchester County, as described by the writer of the "Muskrat Hunting" article in the 1886 (Baltimore) *Sun. Charlie Ewers.*

While still a child, Cook set her to watching his muskrat traps, which compelled her to wade through the water. It happened that she was once sent when she was ill with the measles, and, taking cold from wading in the water in this condition, she grew very sick, and her mother persuaded her master to take her away from Cook's until she could get well.

—Franklin B. Sanborn, (Boston) *Commonwealth*, 1863

❧

"Looking from any point on the edge of the upland, the eye has an unobstructed and almost unlimited range to the horizon over what resembles a vast prairie." This description of South Dorchester County could have been inspired near this point on the Great Marsh.

—(Baltimore) *Sun*, "Muskrat Hunting," February 19, 1886

LEFT: R. Bruce Horsfall, "The Muskrat eating the small white part of the rush," circa 1900. Harriet Tubman trapped these animals using a wooden version of the gum held by Ted Abbott in the photograph on page 111. *Library of Congress.*

BELOW: Muskrat dens on a cold winter's day on the Great Marsh in South Dorchester County. A misstep on a day like this could lead to a dunking in the icy waters of a pothole. *Charlie Ewers.*

The traps are made of boards about six inches wide and three feet long. These are nailed together like an ordinary box trap, the open ends being secured by swinging doors of wire network, fastened to the upper part of both entrances. These doors allow easy ingress to the trap, but, once in, the rat cannot get out without opening the door by pulling it to him, which secret they seem very slow to discover. These traps are put in the leads running from the houses to the water when the tide is at low ebb, and the rats are out feeding. On the return they crawl up the lead, push against one of the wire doors of the trap, which immediately opens toward him....[T]he tide makes up and he is drowned in the trap. By having a number of traps, and watching the tides closely, a trapper can capture a large number in this way.

—*Fur Trade Review*, "Muskrat Hunting," September 1, 1887

⁂

I began trapping muskrats when I was five years old behind my home in Robbins. I trapped a ditchbank there by myself. From my father who was half Indian (who learned from his own brother), I learned most everything about trapping in the marsh. Where to find muskrats. How to tell the difference between good leads (paths) and bad leads. How to read their sign. Where to set your traps.

In the marsh you learned yourself where to step and where not to step. You would get wet. It didn't take you long to learn. If you fell into a hole you were freezing afterwards. You'll learn from that.

—Ted Abbott, trapper, Dorchester County, Maryland

I stepped carelessly into a little ditch. It was only about 10 to 12 inches wide with water only two inches deep, but—alas—the mud under the water was—well—40 feet probably.

—Agate, "A Morning with a Trapper," *Little Corporal Magazine*, February 1873

If he is alive, he is speedily dispatched by a blow on the head from a stick....This blow can be delivered in a certain spot so as to kill the rat quickly and without soiling or in any way injuring the fur.

—Charles Curtis, "Trapping Muskrats," *Popular Science Monthly*, January-June 1917

All furs are best in winter....[F]ur-bearing animals shed their coats, or at least lose the finest and thickest part of their fur as warm weather approaches, and have a new growth of it in the fall to protect them in winter....Beavers and muskrats are not thoroughly prime till about the middle of winter.

—S. Newhouse, *The Trapper's Guide*, 1865

Often in the coldest nights in winter in rain, in snow and sleet, have I got out of my warm bed and sometimes gone as far as three miles to look after my traps.

—Worthington Whittredge, *Autobiography*, 1942

LEFT: Dorchester County trapper Ted Abbott holding an old gum (trap). Speaking about trapping in the coldest months of the year, he recalled, "If you fell into a hole, you were freezing afterwards. You'll learn from that." *Charlie Ewers*.

BELOW: Marion Post Wolcott, "Untitled, possibly related to Spanish trapper hanging muskrats up to dry their fur before skinning. Stretching and drying the pelt follows this," 1941. *Library of Congress*.

[S]he was hired by a woman who, though married and the mother of a family, was still "Miss Susan" to her slaves, as is customary at the South....[S]he had been brought up to believe, and to act upon the belief, that a slave could be taught to do nothing, and *would* do nothing but under the sting of the whip. Harriet...was put to housework without being told how to do anything...."Move these chairs and tables into the middle of the room, sweep the carpet clean, then dust everything, and put them back in their places!" These were the directions given, and Harriet was left alone to do her work.

The whip was in sight on the mantelpiece, as a reminder of what was to be expected if the work was not done well. Harriet fixed the furniture as she was told to do, and swept with all her strength, raising a tremendous dust. The moment she had finished sweeping, she took her dusting cloth, and wiped everything "so you could see your face in 'em, de shone so," in haste to go and set the table for breakfast, and do her other work. The dust which she had set flying only settled down again on chairs, tables, and the piano. "Miss Susan" came in and looked around. Then came the call for Minty....

She drew her up to the table, saying, "What do you mean by doing my work this way, you—!" and passing her finger on the table and piano, she showed her the mark it made through the dust. "Miss Susan, I done sweep and dust jus' as you tole me." But the whip was already taken down, and the strokes were falling on head and face and neck.

—Sarah Hopkins Bradford, *Scenes in the Life of Harriet Tubman*, 1869

Araminta found that [whipping] was usually a morning exercise; so she prepared for it by putting on all the thick clothes she could procure to protect her skin. She made sufficient outcry, however, to convince her mistress that her blows had full effect; and in the afternoon she would take off her wrappings, and dress as well as she could.

—Ednah Dow Cheney, "Moses," *Freedmen's Record*, 1865

Four times this scene was repeated before breakfast, when, during the fifth whipping, the door opened, and "Miss Emily" came in. She was a married sister of "Miss Susan."... Not being able to endure the screams of the child any longer, she came in, took her sister by the arm, and said, "Leave her to me a few moments;" and Miss Susan left the room, indignant. As soon as they were alone, Miss Emily said: "Now, Minty, show me how you do your work."...[S]he took the dusting cloth to wipe off the furniture. "Now stop there," said Miss Emily; "and when it is time to dust, I will call you." When the time came she called her, and explained to her how the dust had now settled, and that if she wiped it off now, the furniture would remain bright and clean. These few words an hour or two before, would have saved Harriet her whippings for that day, as they probably did for many a day after.

—Sarah Hopkins Bradford, *Scenes in the Life of Harriet Tubman*, 1869

ABOVE: L. Prang & Co., "Prang's Aids for Object Teaching—The Kitchen," circa 1874. This kitchen alone would have contained much to learn about for a young girl recently removed from the slave quarters. Tending an entire home could pose almost insurmountable challenges. *Library of Congress*.

It will generally be expected that punishment by whipping should be mentioned among the revolting features of slavery. In a well-regulated southern household, as in a well-ordered family of children, or a good school, the rod is out of sight. It is seldom alluded to; threatenings are rare; but the knowledge on the part of each servant, child, and pupil, that there is a punishment in reserve for the last resort, will have a salutary effect. Southern ladies, when they meet insolence or disobedience in their slaves, have not our easy means of relief in dismissing them at once, and repairing to the intelligence offices for others. They must have them punished, or they must continue to bear with them, as they often do, with long and exemplary patience, shrinking as we should from subjecting them to punishment; or they must sell them, as incorrigible, to the slave trader, which is far worse than chastisement, however severe. In good hands this power is exercised without abuse.

—Nehemiah Adams, *A South-Side View of Slavery*, 1854.

An apologist for slavery from the North who inspired the reply *North-Side View of Slavery* by Benjamin Drew, Nehemiah Adams justified the beatings of enslaved people, equating them with the beating of children in a family and pupils in school. This form of punishment would inflict psychological and physical scars on those children and enslaved people unfortunate enough to receive the blows of Adams's "well-ordered" school or household.

"Show us your mark, Aunt Harriet."...

"My whippin's? Sho'? Dey almost gone."...

After a little more pretense of disinclination, she would draw down her dress and exhibit the cruel weals on neck and shoulders.

"Didn't it hurt awfully"?

"Dey nevah make Harriet Hollah."

—Samuel Hopkins Adams, *Grandfather Stories*, 1947

⚮

While with this woman, after working from early morning till late at night, she was obliged to sit up all night to rock a cross, sick child. Her mistress laid upon her bed with a whip under her pillow, and slept; but if the tired nurse forgot herself for a moment, if her weary head dropped, and her hand ceased to rock the cradle, the child would cry out, and then down would come the whip upon the neck and face of the poor weary creature. The scars are still plainly visible where the whip cut into the flesh. Perhaps her mistress was preparing her, though she did not know it then, by this enforced habit of wakefulness, for the many long nights of travel, when she was the leader and guide of the weary and hunted ones who were escaping from bondage.

—Sarah Hopkins Bradford, *Scenes in the Life of Harriet Tubman*, 1869

"I was only seven years old when I was sent away to take car' of a baby. I was so little dat I had to sit down on de flo' and hev de baby put in my lap. An' dat baby was allus in my lap 'cept when it was asleep, or its mother was feedin' it.

"One mornin' after breakfast she had de baby, an' I stood by de table waitin' till I was to take it; just by me was a bowl of lumps of white sugar. My Missus got into a great quarrel wid her husband; she had an awful temper, an' she would scole an' storm, an' call him all sorts of names. Now you know, Missus, I never had nothing good; no sweet, no sugar, an' dat sugar, right by me, did look so nice, an' my Missus's back was turned to me while she was fightin' wid her husband, so I jes' put my fingers in de sugar bowl to take one lump, an' maybe she heard me, an' she turned an' saw me. De nex' minute she had de raw hide down; I give one jump out of de do', an' I saw dey came after me, but I jes' flew, and dey didn't catch me. I run, an' I run, an' I run, I passed many a house, but I didn't dar' to stop, for dey all knew my Missus an' dey would send me back. By an' by, when I was clar tuckered out, I come to a great big pig-pen. Dar was an ole sow dar, an' perhaps eight or ten little pigs. I was too little to climb into it, but I tumbled ober de high board, an' fell in on de ground; I was so beat out I couldn't stir.

"An' dere, Missus, I stayed from Friday till de nex' Chuesday, fightin' wid dose little pigs for de potato peelin's an' oder scraps dat come down in de trough. De ole sow would push me away when I tried to git her chillen's food, an' I was awful afeard of her. By Chuesday I was so starved I knowed I'd got to go back to my Missus, I hadn't got no whar else to go, but I knowed what was comin'. So I went back."

"And she gave you an awful flogging, I suppose, Harriet?"

"No, Missus, but he did."

—Sarah Hopkins Bradford, *Harriet: The Moses of Her People* (1901 edition)

SUSAN MEREDITH

When I think of Minty Ross, the future Harriet Tubman, working on the Cook farm across the street, my mind goes first to her grandmother, the African-born Modesty. Being picked up in Africa and taken away to America must have been like going to Mars. She didn't know the people she would serve. She didn't understand the language they spoke. And little Minty, too, left her home and her mother to live with strangers in a new world right across this road.

I was a girl who liked to be outside, and I can imagine little Minty going trapping in the marsh. It must have made her stronger. It was one piece of the puzzle that made it possible for her to carry a man over her shoulder to escape his pursuers

Charlie Ewers.

and to serve in a field of battle in the Civil War. Her hard life made her what she was. God makes all of us what we are in that way.

When Minty went to work for Miss Susan, she was beaten because she seemed too stupid to dust the furniture. But Miss Susan's sister Emily knew better: she asked Susan, "Have you taught her?" Perhaps Emily knew that Minty had a mind that was going all the time. When she grew up, Harriet realized that there was no other way but to go to freedom. Her husband asked why anything should be different, but Harriet knew what to do with her life.

As children, we know how words can hurt. Imagine if Minty had believed what people said about her. But she said to herself, "I am not worthless." She knew her life wouldn't amount to anything if she accepted what they told her. She knew that she could change her life.

My mother taught me to say something nice to people no matter how they treated me. I learned from her that words could help heal. She helped me to see that my purpose is to be a bright spot in the lives of others. When life gets hard, I think of Minty and the ways she was hurt as a child. She makes me stronger. She is a bright spot for me.

—SUSAN MEREDITH

Co-owner of Blackwater Paddle and Pedal Adventures and restorer and co-owner of the Bucktown Store

5

A Stunning Blow

WORKING AS A FIELD HAND AND RECEIVING A NEARLY FATAL WOUND

Settled by families sailing up Hall's Branch from the Transquaking River, the crossroads of Bucktown joined roads between Cambridge and Vienna and between the Transquaking and Little Blackwater Rivers. The village supported one or two stores and a blacksmith's shop in the nineteenth century. The creeks and marshes of the area carved out stretches of good farmland that produced food, fodder and fiber. Farmers here could hire enslaved people from neighbors who had more labor than they needed. *Charlie Ewers.*

Soon after she entered her teens she was hired out as a field hand, and it was while thus employed that she received a wound which nearly proved fatal, from the effects of which she still suffers.

—Franklin B. Sanborn, "Harriet Tubman," (Boston) *Commonwealth*, July 17, 1863

⚓

"I was put out again for victuals and clothes to the worst man in the neighborhood, and he set me to breaking flax. My hair had never been combed and it stood out like a bushel basket, and when I'd get through eating I'd wipe the grease off my fingers on my hair, and I expect that there hair saved my life."

—Emma Paddock Telford, *Harriet: The Modern Moses of Heroism and Visions*, circa 1905

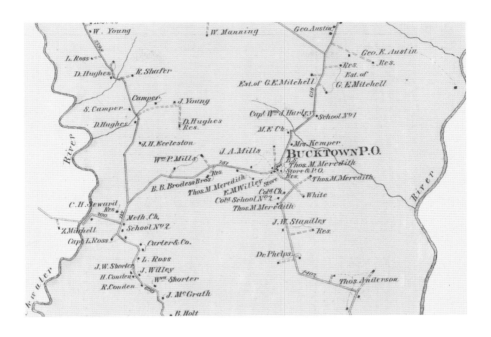

OPPOSITE: Harriet Tubman worked as a hired farm laborer near Bucktown, where wheat, corn and flax grew abundantly and—when there was a surplus—could be transported to city markets by road or river. *Charlie Ewers.*

ABOVE: Simon J. Martenet, "Dorchester County," 1865. The map shows the crossroads of Bucktown in the mid-nineteenth century. *From* Martenet's Atlas of Maryland, *1865.*

LEFT: *Harriet Tubman Underground Railroad Byway Driving Map, Site 17.*

ABOVE: A reflection of Greenbrier Road from a front window of the Bucktown General Store, leading to the Brodess Farm, where Harriet Tubman lived during a fateful period of her life. *Charlie Ewers.*

LEFT: Jean-Francois Millet, "Breaking Flax," 1850–51, illustrating how the flax brake was used, as described by David Pletcher of the Stahlstown Flax Scutching Festival. *The Walters Art Museum.*

Around Buckstown *[sic]*, the country is more elevated, the soil lighter, with a growth of very large oaks and American poplars.

—J.T. Ducatel, "Report of the Geologist," in J.H. Alexander and J.T. Ducatel, *Report of the Engineer and Geologist, in Relation to the New Map, to the Executive of Maryland*, 1836

A fertile farming community surrounds it. Two stores, one M.E. Church and about forty people in ten or twelve dwellings measure the size of that quiet town.

—Elias Jones, *History of Dorchester County, Maryland*, 1902

The third great obstacle which has hitherto stood in the way of an extended cultivation of flax has been the great trouble and annoyance to which the farmer has been compelled to submit, in order to prepare his produce for market.

—The Chevalier Claussen, *The Flax Movement*, 1851

I've prepared flax for more than sixty years, from the time I was a kid. Flax is a useful plant [from which you get oil, as well as fiber]. *Linen from flax wears forever. It is a tough fabric....*

The day for flax scutching would have to be perfect with just the right amount of dryness and sun. You remove the seeds to permit them to dry out. You break the flax by crushing the outer casing of the flax stalks, leaving the fiber behind. We break the flax in two steps with different flax breaks.

Once the flax is broken, we do the scutching, running a scutching paddle against the flax fiber down a board. This further removes pieces of the casing and helps separate the fibers. Then we pull the fibers through the teeth of a hackle so that all of the fibers are separated and combed out. Then it's ready to be spun into thread and woven into cloth.

The breaking was the most important part of the process. You would be really working hard if you did it all day. You needed to do it right to make the rest of the process go smoothly. You wouldn't see many children or women breaking flax. It was mainly a man's job. Often the bigger guys would do it. Even so, my son learned breaking as a kid and now he does it better than me.

Often, you would change positions during the day between breaking, scutching and hackling. When I did hackling very long, I would get bloody hands.

Harriet Tubman had her head on straight to be able to break flax. She probably had to do it over and over until she was good at it. It is not surprising that she was able to do what she accomplished in her life later. It took a tough person to do what she did.

—David Pletcher, chairman, flax demonstration, Flax Scutching Festival, Stahlstown, Pennsylvania

Broken flax and hackle, Bucktown General Store. After breaking and scutching, flax would be run through the hackle several times to remove remaining fragments of the outer casing of the flax plant and separate the fibers for spinning—a difficult and painful step, as described on the following page by Renee Campbell of the Stahlstown Flax Scutching Festival. *Charlie Ewers.*

*I knows how to raise flax. You grow it an' when it is grown you
pull it clean up out of de groun' till it kinder rots. Dey have
what dey call a brake, den it was broke up in dat. De bark waz
de flax. Dey would den put de flax on a hackle, a board wid a
lot of pegs in it. Den dey clean an' string it out till it looks lik
your hair. Dey flax when it came from de hackles wuz ready for
de wheel wur it was spun into thread.*

—Parker Pool, *Slave Narratives*, Vol. 11, North Carolina, Part 2, 1937

It is harder to spin flax than wool for example. The fiber
is hard on your fingers, unlike wool, where the lanolin will
actually soothe your fingers. Sometimes the flax will break on
you. You will get callouses from weaving flax.

—Renee Campbell, volunteer spinner and weaver, Stahlstown Flax Scutching Festival

In the fall of the year, the slaves there work in the evening,
cleaning up wheat, husking corn, etc. On this occasion, one
of the slaves of a farmer named Barrett [*sic, actually Barnett*]
left his work, and went to the village store in the evening. The
overseer followed him, and so did Harriet.

—Franklin B. Sanborn, "Harriet Tubman," the (Boston) *Commonwealth*, July 17, 1863

*I applied all my leisure hours, for several months after this, in
making wooden trays, and such other wooden vessels as were
most in demand. These I traded off, in part, to a store-keeper,
who lived about five miles from the plantation; and for some of
my work I obtained money.*

—Charles Ball, *A Narrative of the Adventures and Life of Charles Ball*, 1837

OPPOSITE: Russell Lee, "Country Store, Wagoner County, Oklahoma," 1939. General store
owners would have a steady traffic of free and enslaved African Americans selling crafts and
items from gardening or gathering and buying tobacco and other consumer items for their
use. *Library of Congress*.

The money...is laid out by the slaves in purchasing such little articles of necessity or luxury, as it enables them to procure. A part is disbursed in payment for sugar, molasses, and sometimes a few pounds of coffee, for the use of the family; another part is laid out for clothes for winter; and no inconsiderable portion of his pittance is squandered away by the misguided slave for tobacco, and an occasional bottle of rum.

[T]he shops or stores are frequently kept at some cross road, or other public place, in or adjacent to a rich district of plantations. To these shops the slaves resort, sometimes with, and at other times, without the consent of the overseer, for the purpose of laying out the little money they get.

—Charles Ball, *A Narrative of the Adventures and Life of Charles Ball*, 1837

"One night I went out with the cook to the store to get some things for the house. I had a shoulder shawl of the mistress's over my head and when I got to the store I was shamed to go in and [saw] the overseer raising up his arm to throw an iron weight at one of the slaves and that was the last I knew."

—Emma Paddock Telford, *Harriet: The Modern Moses of Heroism and Visions*, circa 1905

OPPOSITE: Interior of the store at Bucktown, displaying the many items that would be available at a general store. *Charlie Ewers.*

ABOVE: Scale at the Bucktown General Store. Note the hanging weights such as the one that was thrown at Harriet Tubman. *Charlie Ewers.*

When the slave was found, the overseer swore he should be whipped, and called on Harriet, among others, to help tie him. She refused, and as the man ran away, she placed herself in the door to stop pursuit. The overseer caught up a two-pound weight from the counter and threw it at the fugitive, but it fell short and struck Harriet a stunning blow on the head.

—Franklin B. Sanborn, "Harriet Tubman," the (Boston) *Commonwealth*, July 17, 1863

∾

"That weight struck me in the head and broke my skull and cut a piece of that shawl clean off and drove it into my head. They carried me to the house all bleeding and fainting. I had no bed, no place to lie down on at all, and they lay me on the seat of the loom, and I stayed there all that day and the next, and then next day I went to work again and there I worked with the blood and sweat rolling down my face till I couldn't see."

—Emma Paddock Telford, *Harriet: The Modern Moses of Heroism and Visions*, circa 1905

SLAVE-OWNER SHOOTING A FUGITIVE SLAVE.

TOP: Wilson Armistead, "Slave-Owner Shooting a Fugitive Slave," 1853. Enslaved people feared owners and overseers who abused them with impunity. "The slave is liable to be coerced or punished by the whip, and to be tormented by every species of personal ill-treatment....Nor is any special mandate or express general power necessary for this purpose; it is enough that the inflictor of the violence is set over the slave for the moment, or by the owner or by any of his delegates or sub-delegates, of whatever rank or character." The quote is from antislavery lawyer and parliamentarian James Steven, *The Slavery of the West Indian Colonies Delineated*, 1824, cited by Anti-Slavery Society member William Goodell, *The American Slave Code*, 1852. *Wikipedia*.

BOTTOM: Imagine something similar to this bench to the left of a loom from Furnace Town Historic Site that would have supported the injured Harriet Tubman. *Charlie Ewers*.

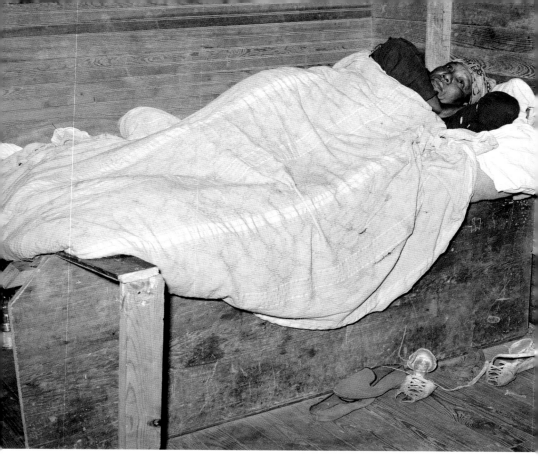

The day's work must be accomplished, whether the head was racked with pain, and the frame was consumed by fever, or not; but the day came at length when poor Harriet could work no more.

—Sarah Hopkins Bradford, *Harriet, the Moses of Her People*, 1897

ABOVE: Russell, Lee, "Negro Woman Sick in Bed in Strawberry Pickers Quarter, Independence, Louisiana," 1939. Harriet Tubman "lay ill a whole winter" recovering from her head injury, which left her with a disability for the rest of her life. *Library of Congress.*

For a long time, her life was despaired of.

—Robert W. Taylor, *Harriet Tubman—The Heroine in Ebony*, 1901

She lay ill a whole winter. Her master offered to sell her for a very low price, and used to bring men to look at her. She heard them discuss the bargain, and lying there while the depressing bartering went on about her.

—Lillie B. Chace Wyman, "Harriet Tubman," *New England Magazine*, 1896

"Dey said dey wouldn't give a sixpence for me," she said.

—Sarah Hopkins Bradford, *Scenes in the Life of Harriet Tubman*, 1869

It was long before she recovered from this, and it has left her subject to a sort of stupor or lethargy at times; coming upon her in the midst of conversation, or whatever she may be doing, and throwing her into a deep slumber, from which she will presently rouse herself, and go on with her conversation or work.

—Franklin B. Sanborn, "Harriet Tubman," the (Boston) *Commonwealth*, July 17, 1863

Still the pressure upon the brain continued, and with the weight half lifted, she would drop off into a state of insensibility, from which even the lash in the hand of a strong man could not rouse her.

—Sarah Hopkins Bradford, *Harriet, the Moses of Her People*, 1897

She cannot remain quiet fifteen minutes without appearing to fall asleep. It is not a refreshing slumber; but a heavy weary condition which exhausts her. She therefore loves great physical activity, and direct heat of the sun, which keeps her blood actively circulating.

—Ednah Dow Cheney, "Moses," *The Freedmen's Record*, March 1865

The attacks, which...are particularly frequent when patient is not actively engaged, also occur in the midst of hard physical labor....[T]he patient, in the hope that hard labor might prevent the occurrence of the attacks, accepted employment as a longshoreman....Even work of this kind did not influence the occurrence of the seizures. As regards the character of these seizures, the patient...can give but little information; he says that his eyes grow heavy and, notwithstanding strenuous efforts to prevent it, they close and he sleeps; he has no further premonition of the approaching attack, and during it is perfectly unconscious.

—George W. Jacoby, MD, "Periodical Sleep Seizures of an Epileptic Nature," *New York Medical Journal*, May 20, 1893.

This article reports a case that may have been similar to what is thought to be Harriet Tubman's temporal lobe epilepsy.

JAY MEREDITH

Bucktown was quite a hub of commerce in the mid-1800s. Schooners landed down the road at Bestpitch. Here there were two stores and a blacksmith's shop serving the farms in the area. Colonel James Wallace said that the land between the Little Blackwater and Transquaking Rivers was the Garden of Eden of this part of the Shore. The house next door goes back to the 1790s and would have been seen

Charlie Ewers.

by Harriet Tubman, when she was hired for the harvest nearby.

As farms became larger, prosperous landowners like Thomas Barnett depended on hiring out overseers and enslaved people. As hires, enslaved people sometimes had more of a chance to earn extra money to spend at the local store. In that situation, Harriet Tubman goes to work for Thomas Barnett as an innocent young woman, doing her jobs inside and outside the house. What happened to her here was a major turning point in her life.

Close to death after being hit, she is changed—considered "damaged goods" by people who might hire her. No longer considered fit to be a house servant, she's given difficult tasks like logging along the swamps and trapping in the marshes. In the years following her injury, she learns survival in a whole new way. As if it was ordained, her strength and persistence grows. She decides to escape to freedom when it appears that her family will be sold and separated.

My family goes back four generations here but sold much of its property when my people moved to the city. When the store closed in 1972 and began to deteriorate, we knew that it had to be restored, using much of our own money to pay for what the grants didn't.

We can only begin to imagine what Harriet Tubman went through. We've hunted here, so we know how dark it can get and what sounds come out of the swamp at night. We respect her for what she did. With so much against her, her being a young, enslaved woman, she accomplished her desire. You cannot look at what she did without admiring her. She motivates us all.

—JAY MEREDITH,
Restorer and co-owner of the Bucktown Store

6

The Rudest Labors

HIRING HER TIME AND HAULING TIMBER

This spot on the upper Blackwater River is where Stewart's Canal joined Parson's Creek, making it easier to bring out timber by water at least partway to the shipyards and sawmills of Madison and Church Creek. Working for her father, Ben Ross, Harriet Tubman may have used her team of steers to drag timber to Stewart's Canal or perhaps even pulled logs or barges along the canal. The wood in this area was so valuable that a second canal, looping from Corsey's Creek to Madison, began to take shape. It was not completed, however, for several years after Harriet Tubman left Dorchester County, sometime between 1865 and 1877. The two canals brought salty Chesapeake Bay tides inland that washed into the upper Blackwater River, creating the "ghost forests" near the waterways. *Charlie Ewers*.

ABOVE: Harriet Tubman did housework on the Stewart holdings at Madison, scene of shipyards, lumber mills and later docks for oystering and crabbing. *Charlie Ewers.*

LEFT: *Harriet Tubman Underground Railroad Byway Driving Map, Site 9.*

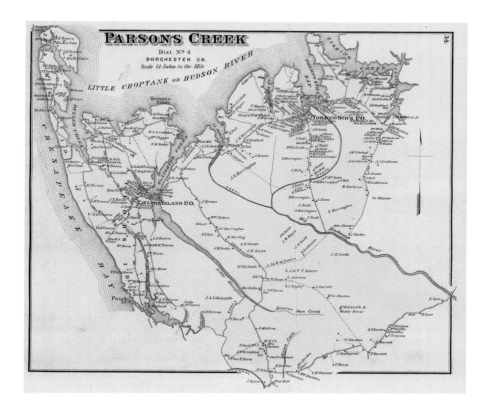

[S]he lived for five or six years with John Stewart, where at first she worked in the house, but afterward "hired her time."

—Franklin B. Sanborn, "Harriet Tubman," the (Boston) *Commonwealth*, July 17, 1863

ABOVE: Lake, Griffing & Stevenson, "Parsons Creek," 1877. This map shows both Stewart's Canal, its later Corsey Creek extension and the village of Madison. This district was the center of Harriet Tubman's life in the years before she left Dorchester County for good. *From* An Illustrated Atlas of Talbot & Dorchester Counties, Maryland, *1877.*

Julian Vannerson, "James A. Stewart, Representative from Maryland," 1859. Harriet Tubman found work with the Stewart family, likely with the help of her father, Ben Ross. The brothers John T. Stewart (to whom Harriet Tubman was hired out) and James A. Stewart—who "always took an interest in boating [and] built a number of bay crafts and coasting vessels himself and at one time owned a great deal of vessel property," according to "Death of Judge Stewart," the (Easton) *Star-Democrat*, April 8, 1879—would come to profit from Harriet Tubman's strength and grit bringing out timber by a team of steers to the family lumber mills and shipyards. In doing this work, Harriet Tubman was "hired out" from Edward Brodess. Dr. Anthony Thompson, who had known Harriet Tubman's family from the days when his father married the widowed mother of Edward Brodess, "stood for her" by entering into the contract for hire with Edward Brodess, knowing that Stewart or Harriet herself would have paid Brodess each year to keep the contract. *Library of Congress.*

Dr. Thompson, son of her master's guardian, "stood for her," that is, was her surety for the payment of what she owed.

—Franklin B. Sanborn, "Harriet Tubman," the (Boston) *Commonwealth*, July 17, 1863

"Yes, sir, I invest in niggers; that's what I do; and I hire them out, sir,—hire them out. Why, sir, if a man has a knowledge of human nature, knows where to buy and when to buy, and watches his opportunity, he gets a better percentage on his money that way than any other....Say, now, that you give one thousand dollars for a man,—and I always buy the best sort, that's economy,—well, and he gets—put it at the lowest figure—ten dollars a month wages, and his living. Well, you see there, that gives you a pretty handsome sum for your money."

—Mr. Jekyl, in Harriet Beecher Stowe, *Dred: A Tale of the Great Dismal Swamp*, 1856

But were more slaves to be kept than were needed to cultivate the land economically, where no crops are raised except maize and wheat, the surplus hands would detract as much from the profits of a plantation as the keeping of extra hands on a farm in a Free State would assuredly be unprofitable.

—Robert Russel, *North America, Its Agriculture & Climate*, 1857

PUBLIC HIRING OF NEGROES

Will be hired at "Wakefield," the farm in Hanover County, next adjoining Mr. Geo. W. Doswell's, on FRIDAY, the 31st day of the present month (December), about forty Negroes, consisting of men and women, boys and girls.

They will be hired as farm hands and house servants—in no instance to labor on works of internal improvement, or in occupations considered hazardous; and with the further express understanding that they are not to be re-hired by those who hire them publically, without the written consent of the undersigned.

Bonds with approved security will be required in every instance.

S.W. Richardson

Ex'or of Mrs. Judith Smith, dec'd.

Richmond Dispatch, December 25, 1858

Aug, 23rd, 1864
Mr. J.2.A. Haddaway,
Dear Sir,
Albert will take Ellen up to you this afternoon to serve you until the end of the present year. The wages will be at the rate of $22.50 a year, the amt. I am to pay Mr. J.W. Martin for the girl. She will go to you with a full supply of clothing, and whatever she may need at the end of the year you must furnish her with. You will excuse me for being explicit when I tell you I have had no little trouble in this way. Ellen's clothes: 2 shirts, 2 petticoats, 4 frocks, 2 aprons, one pr. shoes, 2 pr. farm stockings (to be sent), one cloak.
Yrs.
Nichs. Willis

James Dawson, ed., *100 Years of Change on the Eastern Shore*, 2014

She employed her duties to her master faithfully, but in the caverns of her untutored mind there ever burned the fire which was the heritage of her warlike and liberty loving lineage.

—Frank C. Drake, "The Moses of Her People: The Amazing Life Work of Harriet Tubman," *New York Herald*, September 22, 1907

She was employed on the plantation in various ways. When she was sent to the bedrooms to make up the beds, she would beat up the feather beds, make believe that she was working hard, and when she had blown them up she would throw herself in the middle of them.

—Mrs. William Tatlock, "Interview with Earl Conrad," August 15, 1939

"JARVIS HILL" RESIDENCE AND FARM OF Wᵐ G. LECOMPTE DIST. N°7 DORCHESTER CO. MD.

TOP: The Dr. Benjamin Smith house is thought to be the oldest standing home in Madison, built in the second quarter of the nineteenth century. Imagine this house serving as the anchor of a thriving community at the meeting of Madison Bay to the north and White Marsh Road to the south. *Charlie Ewers.*

BOTTOM: "Jarvis Hill," from Lake, Griffing & Stevenson, 1877. This home may suggest the sort of estate where Harriet Tubman worked for John T. Stewart as a household servant. She later worked outdoors cutting and transporting timber with her father—perhaps seeing the hard labor as a way to ward off narcolepsy, as described by Dr. Jacoby in the previous chapter. *From* An Illustrated Atlas of Talbot & Dorchester Counties, Maryland, *1877.*

The planters towards the bay build their houses on some
eminence, remote from the miasmata of low marshy grounds
and stagnant waters. Their dwellings...are mostly of frame,
generally painted brown or yellow. Some have brick dwellings.
At a little distance from the dwellings of the planters are
the huts or quarters of their slaves. The number of slaves
on a plantation is always in proportion to the wealth of the
planter. Some have five, some have ten, some have fifteen;
There are some who have a great many more.

—Joseph Scott, *Geographical Description of the States of Maryland and
Delaware*, 1807

The labor of the horse and the ox, the lifting of barrels of flour and other heavy weights were given to her; and powerful men often stood astonished to see this woman perform feats of strength from which they shrunk incapable.

—Sarah Hopkins Bradford, *Harriet, the Moses of Her People*, 1886

As Harriet grew older she became a marvelous specimen of physical womanhood, and before she was 19 years old was a match for the strongest man on the plantation....He [John T. Stewart] would often exhibit her feats of strength to his friends as one of the sights of his place. She could lift huge barrels and draw a loaded stone boat like an ox.

—Frank C. Drake, "The Moses of Her People: The Amazing Life Work of Harriet Tubman," New York Herald, September 22, 1907

The principle [*sic*] article of carriage on the [proposed Little Blackwater–Choptank] canal would be, for the present, wood to be used in fuel. Of this, immense quantities could be furnished by the yet untouched forests...and a fresh growth every twenty years would rival for perhaps a century the abundance of the first clearing.

—J.H. Alexander, "Engineer's Report," in *Report on the New Map of Maryland*, 1836

OPPOSITE: Joseph John Kirkbride, "Negro Ox Team" 1884–91. Whether free or enslaved, African Americans would save from additional earnings to acquire teams of "steers" or oxen to profit from the thriving timber and cordwood industry. *Library of Congress.*

I admit that the present licentious manner of treating our forests, would require a considerable time to destroy them in the interior; but those remaining on the margin of rivers and near cities, where most valuable and useful, will in a very short time vanish before the cultivators of the soil. We shall then be compelled, at an enormous expense, to send far into the country to procure timber for our public works, all which inconveniences are now easily anticipated and prevented.

—Peter Guillet, *Timber Merchant's Guide*, 1823

Lumbering and shipbuilding, so extensively carried on for more than 150 years, is an industry of the county that has suffered the greatest decline. Vast tracts of oak and pine timber, once so plentiful and cheap, are now almost exhausted. As early as 1735, vessel building was active on both the Choptank and Nanticoke Rivers....Since 1738 many Bay and seacoasting vessels have been built on all the navigable rivers within and bounding the county, and hundreds of cargoes of ship timber have been sent to Baltimore and Eastern cities of the United States for shipbuilding. A much greater bulk of building lumber for general purposes has been shipped out of the county. Forty years ago shipbuilding was a prosperous enterprise at Cambridge, Church Creek, Loomtown, Taylor's Island and on the Nanticoke and Northwest Fork Rivers. Now only at two places in the county are vessels extensively built—Brooks' Yard, near Madison, and Linthicum's, at Church Creek.

—Elias Jones, *History of Dorchester County Maryland*, 1902

OPPOSITE, TOP: "Holland—woman drawing canal boat," circa 1910–15. In demonstrating her strength to John T. Stewart's friends, Harriet Tubman also may have pulled a canal skiff laden with stone or—more likely—timber from the Stewart holdings. *Library of Congress.*

OPPOSITE, BOTTOM: Built from the 1830s to the 1840s, Stewart's Canal entered the Little Choptank River at this point, where Parson's Creek originally would have flowed. The island in the center (which also can be seen in the *Illustrated Atlas*, on page 139) perhaps helped with the transfer of logs and cordwood from canalboats to schooners to supply the shipyards and sawmills of Madison and Church Creek. *Charlie Ewers.*

INSET: *Harriet Tubman Underground Railroad Byway Driving Map, Site 10.*

Frequently Harriet worked for her father, who was a timber inspector, and superintended the cutting and hauling of great quantities of timber for the Baltimore shipyards. Stewart, his temporary master, was a builder, and for the work of Ross used to receive as much as five dollars a day sometimes, he being a superior workman. While engaged with her father, she would cut wood, haul logs, etc. Her usual "stint" was half a cord of wood in a day.

—Franklin B. Sanborn, "Harriet Tubman," the (Boston) *Commonwealth*, July 17, 1863

MONA, ALCAEA, AND MERLIN, AUGUST 8, 1892.

We observed a few days since a most splendid new vessel, the model and workmanship of which would do credit to our Baltimore ship carpenters. We learned that she was built at Tobacco Stick [Madison] by Mr. George Davis and is intended for the West India trade. If this may be taken as a specimen of what our friends at Tobacco Stick can do in the way of shipbuilding, they need not be ashamed to run their vessels into our port for a cargo.

—(Baltimore) *Sun*, "A Beautiful Craft," May 22, 1841

OPPOSITE: *"Ramona, Alcaea,* and *Merlin,"* 1892. These sporting schooner-yachts under sail suggest the workhorses of Chesapeake Bay that hailed from ports such as Madison and carried not only cordwood and timber but also salt, coal, stone, oysters, bulk grain and canned goods. *Library of Congress.*

ABOVE: "Shipbuilding was long one of the industries for which Dorchester was noted." *From* Dorchester County—A Pictorial History, *1977.*

[She earned] money enough in a year, beyond what she paid her master, "to buy a pair of steers," worth forty dollars. The amount exacted of a woman for her time was fifty or sixty dollars—of a man, one hundred to one hundred and fifty dollars.

—Franklin B. Sanborn, "Harriet Tubman," the (Boston) *Commonwealth*, July 17, 1863

ABOVE: "Logging Removal by Oxcart," circa 1910. Harriet Tubman's investment in steers to pull timber out of the woods would have served her well through their sure footing in the muddy terrain of Dorchester County. *Georgia Studies Images*.

We used ox teams to get the pilings out to the nearest water so that you could float them in. The ox teams were so slow that you always tried to haul them to a landing somewhere on some creek or ditch. Why we even dug some places, and you had to do that all by hand with just a shovel or spade. The oxen were mighty good in the woods, but they were so slow that you had to shorten the distance every way you could.

Them oxen are just so slow, but they can get around in the woods and in the marsh. They've got feet just like a duck; it spreads out.

—Hal Roth, *Conversations in a Country Store*, 1995

Oxen are so unspeakably difficult to manage: it is impossible to back them, insanity to turn them, utter exasperation to hasten them; the only thing they do with any facility is to stop; yet they must be swayed by a touch 'twixt the ears from a long, slender blue-birch gad with a leather lash.

They have a disagreeable way of starting off on a trot unexpectedly, particularly on warm April days, when wild natural impulses, mad longings for forest freedom and life without toil take possession of them at the delicious smell of the spring greenwood, causing them to suddenly lash the neap with their tails and rush frantically for the woods.

—Mary Dean, "Satyrs and Sylvan Boys," *Lippencott's Monthly Magazine*, August 1875

With my iron-wood lever I now lifted with the men; now ran to fasten the chain on a log...now seized the goad, and, with genuine boyish pride, exercised my authority over the oxen, wondering that such huge animals should be so obsequious to my gee, haw, whoa! If ever boy lived on enchanted ground, I did.

—Pharcellus Church, *Mapleton*, 1853

It is not a problem for smaller persons to drive oxen. Harriet Tubman had to do this to survive. She had the physical strength and attitude.

—Steve Matthias

ABOVE: Jim, the off ox, farthest away from the driver; Jack, the nigh ox, nearest the driver; and Steve Matthias at the Carroll County Farm Museum. The off ox takes its lead from the nigh ox, which has the most experience following the driver. *Charlie Ewers.*

I began working with the boys [oxen] when they were six months old. I was not afraid of them. They think that I am the boss, so they won't push me around.

The oxen are born to work and they love to do it. Still, they are always testing you. You need to keep their respect with your attitude.

I hate to use the stick. I don't want them to be afraid of me. However, there are days when they don't want to work, or one of them is lazy. Then I need to make them work.

—Steve Matthias, teamster, Carroll County Farm Museum, with Jim (off ox, pictured on left) and Jack (nigh ox, pictured on right)

Generally, however, they work with me for their well-being, security and food. I'm with them when they eat. When I holler, they come running for their meal. They know that I will protect them. I trim their hooves once a year. They are smart enough to know that I am doing things in their best interests, so they will do what I say. Late in the day, I praise them for a job well done.

Their hooves are good for getting through mud. I just took them through the mud to get here. They did better than me. And they will grip the mud better than a horse.

—Steve Matthias

The horns of the boys were daunting, but you become aware of them. Working the yoke makes them a bit more distant, since you are not as close to them. However, you can bop them on the nose with the goad if you need to. I'd rather warn them, though. I would rather keep the boys satisfied. You want to bond with them. I'll talk to them whenever I am near them.

It took me a while to get good with the boys. You always have to be on your game. They'll act up if you don't. You need animal sense.

—Joanne Morvay Weant, manager and teamster, Carroll County Farm Museum

Every teamster will have his or her own style, but the boys must know what needs to be done. You need the courage and commitment. You have to be here with the boys at night.

To work the boys, you need to know how to carry yourself and to have the right tone of voice. I try to get in front of them. If I throw away my goad, they will stop. It's a command.

Once they ran fifty yards away from me. Well, I drove them right back. I was the boss, after all. You are there to help them survive.

—Scott Holniker, curator and teamster, Carroll County Farm Museum

As a teamster, Harriet Tubman would have been proud to own her team. She would have bonded with them. She depended on them to do the work.

Women are always the strongest people on the farm. That would have been so with Harriet Tubman. Developing a skill set with her oxen would have given her confidence. But even before she did that, she had to be confident in herself.

—Joanne Morvay Weant, manager and teamster, Carrol County Farm Museum

OPPOSITE, TOP: Jack, the nigh ox. *Charlie Ewers.*

OPPOSITE, BOTTOM: Scott Holniker, Jim and Steve Matthias. *Charlie Ewers.*

TOM AND KATE BRADSHAW

Tom: I started in the timber business at the Spicer Lumber Company in 1985. After working there for twelve years, I went on to another job in the transportation industry for another number of years. Back in the summer I began working for a timber harvester hauling timber. That brought me back to the woods.

Charlie Ewers.

Back in the day, you did most of your work in the woods in winter. You marked your trees for cutting in spring, but you cut them in winter when you had labor available after the crops were in.

There is something special about being in the woods in the winter on a day like today. You still will see some birds and squirrels. You might see a bald eagle. You will almost always have peace and solitude. It drowns out the noise of the world and gives you a mental break.

Kate: When we kids were younger, we would go out in the truck with Dad. It was a great time for father-daughter talks. Dad would ask me, "What do you want to be when you grow up? Where do you want to go in life?"

Tom: I also remember walking in these woods as a child. It was my playground out here.

As a child I would learn from my family about how they used to log these woods. In the day they would do a select cut. They would look at the trees, decide which trees to cut, bring down the trees with a

crosscut saw and drag them out with a team of mules or oxen to the mill that was located in the tract of timber they were cutting.

Today, most of the mills are gone. Wood from other places is cheaper than local timber. There is more red tape for us. It's a dying industry here.

People tell you, "Don't cut that tree," as if it were a human being. But the trees you leave to grow old get problems like this oak here. As you can see it has some limbs that appear to have died. God gave us these trees to build homes and boats. You can do this in a responsible way.

KATE: When you cut down trees, you don't kill them all forever. You can see the new trees here that grow in place of the old. In the old days, people were responsible in what they did. They did not waste wood. They used everything. Even the slabs were used to fuel the steam engines and to burn for firewood.

TOM: Thinking about Kate here being with me, I know that Harriet Tubman had a close relationship with her father when she worked in the woods. She was willing to learn from him, and he took pride in her work.

KATE: Harriet Tubman must have felt a special competence working with her father. There she was doing a job for him that a woman normally wouldn't do.

TOM: She did hard, but honest, work. It probably helped her clear her head from the difficult things in her life.

KATE: Being out there in the woods working with her father was something she hadn't experienced for most of her life. She would not want to be separated from her family again.

—Former Councilman Tom Bradshaw, Dorchester County,
and his daughter Kate Bradshaw, student at Salisbury University

7

Confidence in the Word of God

POSSESSED OF STRONG FAITH AND
SUSTAINED BY JESUS

A clearing such as this may give us an idea of two forms of African American worship that were practiced outdoors. Camp meetings were annual events where Black and white people from across the area would spend the week living in family "tents" (often simple shanties) and engaging in worship, hymn singing and fellowship. When the church balconies where they normally sat were given over to white worshippers, African Americans would worship in outdoor services in church yards or clearings, conducted by white or Black preachers. *Charlie Ewers*.

When going on these journeys she often lay alone in the forests all night. Her whole soul was filled with awe of the mysterious Unseen Presence, which thrilled her with such depths of emotion, that all other care and fear vanished. Then she seemed to speak with her Maker "as a man talketh with his friend;" her childlike petitions had direct answers, and beautiful visions lifted her up above all doubt and anxiety into serene trust and faith. No man can be a hero without this faith in some form; the sense that he walks not in his own strength, but leaning on an almighty arm. Call it fate, destiny, what you will, Moses of old, Moses of to-day, believed it to be Almighty God.

—Ednah Dow Cheney, "Moses," *The Freedmen's Record*, March 1865

[Enslaved people] may go to the places of worship used by the whites; but they like their own meetings better.

—*Narrative of the Life of Moses Gandy*, 1843

At the close of a thrilling selection she arose and commenced to speak in a hesitating voice....Soon she was shouting, and so were others also. She possessed such endurance, vitality, and magnetism, that I inquired and was informed it was Harriet Tubman—the "Underground Railroad Moses...."

Service ended, I greeted her. She said, "Are you save?" I gave an affirmative reply. She remarked: "Glory to God," and shouted again.

—James E. Mason, "Pays Tribute to Harriet Tubman," *Auburn Advertiser-Journal*, June 6, 1914

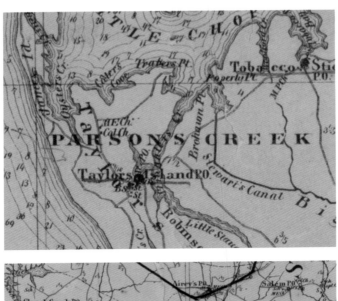

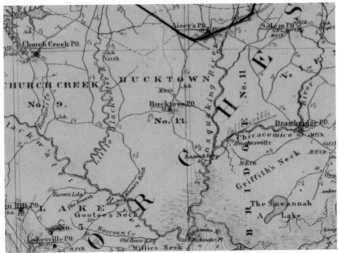

TOP: Lane's church as "Col Ch" in Simon J. Martenet, "Dorchester County," 1866, was an African American congregation that arose after Harriet Tubman left Dorchester. Harriet Tubman and her parents may have attended church services in the "slave gallery" of the local Bethlehem Methodist Episcopal Church on Taylor's Island, located not far from Lane Methodist Episcopal Church. *From* Martenet's Atlas of Maryland, *1865.*

BOTTOM: (Old) Hughes Church as "Col Ch" in Simon J. Martenet, "Dorchester County," 1866, was another African American congregation that arose after Harriet Tubman's time in Dorchester. Harriet Tubman and her parents may have attended church services at Scott's Methodist Episcopal Church in Bucktown, a few miles away from Hughes Church. *From* Martenet's Atlas of Maryland, *1865.*

Methodism came into this country, and found slavery
entrenched in its laws and institutions. Its preachers
proclaimed a gospel of regeneration, of love to God, of
personal knowledge of forgiveness of sins, the witness of
the Holy Ghost, of love to neighbors....It turned out the old
man and let in the new. White and black shared in the new
life. Down in the cabin, up in the "great house," alike were
heard the shouts of joy over this newfound pearl of great
price. Tears of joy coursed down the ebony and ivory cheek,
as each spoke of redeeming love. Melted by this divine fire,
fused into one spirit, there came to heart, to conscience,
to understanding, as the white clasped the black hand with
loving grip, the whispered voice of an inner consciousness,
"surely we be brethren."

—John Braden, "Introduction," in L.M. Heygood, *The Colored Man in the
Methodist Episcopal Church*, 1890

ABOVE: "Directing the Wanderer in the Right Way," in *The History of the Negro Church* by
Carter G. Woodson. In the early years of Methodism, African Americans often were spiritual
guides in Methodist prayer meetings, such as the gathering that led to the conversion of
Reverend Levi Scott, the first Delmarva-born bishop of the Methodist Episcopal Church. *From*
The History of the Negro Church, *1921.*

If God honored the blacks with his Spirit's presence, filling them with joy and peace, enabling them to show forth the power of a Christian life in the fruits of holy living; if he anointed more than one black Harry [Hosier] "to preach good tidings upon the meek, to proclaim the acceptable year of the Lord," and honored their ministry in awaking and saving souls, is it a matter of wonder that there should be the conviction in the minds of Methodists that these slaves are men like ourselves? If men, then they are our neighbors; if our neighbors, then we must love them as ourselves. If we love them as men— as ourselves—then slavery, as it exists here, is wrong.

—John Braden, "Introduction," in L.M. Heygood, *The Colored Man in the Methodist Episcopal Church*, 1890

[I]t is evident that race lines were not as severely drawn as they have been since....Here is a prayer-meeting, conducted mostly by Christian ladies, in the house of a colored member of our Church, on the strictest principles of our exclusive love-feast and class meeting system of the olden day. From that state of things this nation has had a fearful blacksliding up to 1860, when God, in his anger, draped our northern and southern homes in darkest mourning, and spread desolation over our land.

—James Mitchell, *The Life and Times of Levi Scott*, 1885

I rode ten miles and delivered a message from the Lord to a waiting audience—the Master assisted, and seven individuals, white and colored, prostrated themselves for prayer.

—Jarena Lee, *Journal*, 1849. Jarena Lee was an itinerant African American evangelist who preached at churches, camp meetings and other gatherings in the early 1800s.

[W]e have driven off from the M.E. Church thousands of colored persons by our cold neglect....As a general rule, they are not desired in our fine churches. And they know the fact as well as we do. Even the portion of the galleries allotted to them they must resign to the whites frequently on Quarterly Meeting occasions, when the latter are crowded for room. On the other hand, if more colored people are present than can be seated in the gallery, and the lower floor, reserved for the whites, is not half full, they must leave the church without hearing the Gospel, though they may be standing on the brink of eternity.

—John Dixon Long, *Pictures of Slavery in Church and State*, 1857

At first, there was but one front entrance, the gallery being reached by a flight of stairs on either side of it....But owing to the colored people and others crowding down out of the gallery when the lower congregation would be making its exit, these flights of stairs were removed and the two lower front windows were taken out and doors inserted in their place, so that the gallery might be entered and vacated by means of them.

—Reverend W.W.W. Wilson, pastor, Fredericka Methodist Church, 1885, in Allen B. Clark and Jane Herson, *New Light on Old Barratt's*, 1984

LEFT: A. Haffy, "Mrs. Jarena Lee, Preacher of the AME Church." Jarena Lee traveled widely throughout the Delmarva Peninsula and inspired Methodist worshippers Black and white. *From* Religious Experience and Journal of Mrs. Jarena Lee, *1836.*

BELOW: The gallery at Bethlehem Methodist Episcopal Church, which may have seated free and enslaved African American worshippers until the original Lane Methodist Episcopal Church was built. *Charlie Ewers.*

The preacher was always sure of a sympathetic and appreciative audience in the rear. Many a timid, trembling messenger was inspirited and saved from disastrous failure by the demonstrative prayers and sympathies of the colored part of the congregation.

—Robert Todd, *Methodism in the Peninsula*, 1886

We went to the white church on Sunday, up in the slave gallery where the slaves worshipped sometimes. The gallery was overcrowded with ours and slaves from other plantations. [T]here was once an old colored man who attended....He had the habit of saying Amen. A member of the church said to him, "John, if you don't stop hollowing Amen you can't come to church." He got so full of the Holy Ghost he yelled out Amen....[The congregation] told him to come when and as often as he wanted.

—Annie Young Henson, in Federal Writers' Project, Vol. VIII (Maryland), 1937

The colored population greatly enjoyed those exercises as they crowded the old galleries, and had but the bare privilege of singing a hymn or two at the close of our exercises each evening.

—Adam Wallace (ed. by Joseph F. diPaolo), *My Business Was to Fight the Devil*, 1998

OPPOSITE, TOP: Alfred T. Scott, Barratt's Chapel, Kent County, Delaware, 1850. This view of Barratt's Chapel shows the common entrance for the entire congregation. *Barratt's Chapel and Museum of Methodism.*

OPPOSITE, BOTTOM: This contemporary photograph of Barratt's Chapel shows how, in the decade between 1850 and 1860, the windows on either side of the original entrance were made into doors that led to the upstairs gallery stairs segregating African American worshippers. *Charlie Ewers.*

I was so tired and sleepy that I had to lay down. That night passed away [at the camp meeting] with me not like any other night I have known in this world. My wife and myself had a tent to ourselves where we lay with the rain pouring on us, while it was lightning and thundering most awfully, and the poor black people singing and shouting as loud as thunder in all the rain.

—William Colbert, *Journal*, May 1807

ABOVE: This interior photograph of Barratt's Chapel shows part of the U-shaped gallery, generally used by African American worshippers. Even then, the crowds of worshippers would be so great that, according to Reverend Andrew Manship, *Thirteen Years' Experience in the Itinerancy*, 1856, "It was deemed proper to request the coloured people to vacate the gallery for the whites." On the 1842 occasion mentioned in *Thirteen Years*, Reverend Manship, a fledgling minister preaching to the African American congregants on a wagon in the shade of the church grounds, found his voice as a preacher through the enthusiasm of the worshippers. *Charlie Ewers.*

When quite young [Harriet] lived with a pious mistress; but the slaveholder's religion did not prevent her from whipping the young girl for every slight or fancied fault....When invited into family prayers, she preferred to stay on the landing, and pray for herself; "and I prayed to God," she says, "to make me strong and able to fight, and that's what I allers prayed for ever since."

—Ednah Dow Cheney, "Moses," *The Freedmen's Record*, March 1865

Ben *[Ross, father of Harriet Tubman]* did not stop here, he went on to speak of the religious character of his master, and also to describe him physically; he was a Methodist preacher, and had been "pretending to preach for twenty years." Then the fact that a portion of their children had been sold to Georgia by this master was referred to with much feeling by Ben and his wife; likewise the fact that he had stinted them for food and clothing, and led them a rough life generally, which left them no room to believe that he was anything else than "a wolf in sheep's clothing."

—William Still, "Benjamin Ross, and His Wife Harriet," *The Underground Rail Road*, 1871

"*When I think of all the groans and tears and prayers I've heard on the plantations, and remember that God is a prayer-hearing God, I feel that his time is drawing near.*"

—Harriet Tubman, in Ednah Dow Cheney, "Moses," *The Freedmen's Record*, March 1865

"Would your marster allow you to hold prayer-meeting on his place?"

"No, my child; if old marster heard us singing and praying he would come out and make us stop. One time, I remember, we all were having a prayer-meeting in my cabin, and marster came up to the door and hollered out, 'You, Charlotte, what's all that fuss in there?' We all had to hush up for that night.... Marster used to say God was tired of us all hollering to him at night....He did not want us to pray, but we would have our little prayer-meeting anyhow. Sometimes when we met to hold our meetings we would put a big wash-tub full of water in the middle of the floor to catch the sound of our voices when we sung. When we all sung we would march around and shake each other's hands, and we would sing easy and low, so marster could not hear us."

—Octavia Rogers, *House of Bondage*, 1890

ABOVE: George Cruikshank, in Harriet Beecher Stowe, "Prayer Meeting in Uncle Tom's Cabin." In response to their prayer meetings being supervised by a white clergyman or forbidden altogether, enslaved African Americans would hold their meetings at night—sometimes in secret locations. *From* Uncle Tom's Cabin, *1852.*

A good many of us went from the meeting to a brother's cabin, where we began to express our joy in happy songs. The palace of General Dudley was only a little way off, and he soon sent over a slave with orders to stop our noise, or he would send the patrolers upon us. We then stopped our singing, and spent the remainder of the night in talking, rejoicing, and praying. It was a night of very great happiness to me.

—Thomas H. Jones, *Narrative and Personal Experience of Uncle Tom Jones*, 1854

[W]e had scarcely got to work—good work, simply teaching a few colored children how to read the gospel of the Son of God—when in rushed a mob....They were armed with sticks and other missiles and drove us off, commanding us never again to meet for such a purpose. One of this pious crew told me that as for me, I wanted to be another Nat. Turner, and that, if I did not look out, I should get as many balls in me as Nat. did into him. Thus ended the Sabbath-school.

—*Life and Times of Frederick Douglass*, 1881

Sunday schools that taught literacy, as well as Black church services, were suppressed in the native land of Harriet Tubman—especially during rumors of insurrections. This suppression reflected the long afterlife of the rebellion of Nat Turner, who was thought to have embarked on his path of insurrection because of his self-taught literacy and religious beliefs.

[I]f I had not witnessed the fears and cowardice of men of the highest standing, I could not have believed that [rumors of false insurrections] could be the fact. There are men in the slave States, who neither fear God nor regard the white man, that act like nerveless women at the very mention of a slave insurrection. Their imaginations take fire, and they see a "Nat Turner" in every negro boy. On the merest rumor, many of the negroes are taken up and beaten unmercifully, and, for the sake of being let down, confess to any lie that may be suggested; just as the poor creatures of New England confessed to witchcraft in order to mitigate their punishment.

—John Dixon Long, *Pictures of Slavery in Church and State*, 1857

ABOVE: "Horrid Massacre in Virginia." The impact of Nat Turner's Rebellion on the slave-holding states included curbs on African American worship and Sunday schools, arising from Nat Turner's religious beliefs and his literacy. *From* Authentic and Impartial Narrative of the Tragical Scene which Was Witnessed in Southampton County, *1831.*

[A]s it had been said of me in my childhood by those by whom I had been taught to pray, both white and black...that I had too much sense to be raised, and if I was I would never be of any use to any one as a slave. Now finding I had arrived to man's estate, and was a slave, and these revelations being made known to me, I began to direct my attention to this great object, to fulfil the purpose for which, by this time, I felt assured I was intended.

—Thomas R. Gray, *The Confessions of Nat Turner*, 1831

Formerly slaves were allowed to have religious meetings of their own; but after the insurrection which I spoke of before, they were forbidden to meet even for worship. Often they are flogged, if they are found singing or praying at home....A number of slaves went privately into the wood to hold meetings; when they were found out, they were flogged, and each was forced to tell who else was there.

—Moses Gandy, *Narrative of the Life of Moses Gandy*, 1843

[I]n a beautiful grove of woods, I attempted to preach for my colored brethren....While singing the first hymn, a gentleman... came riding by in his carriage, and seeing the congregation, concluded to stop and listen to the sermon. His mare had a young colt, and a saucy fellow he was too....When we knelt in prayer, he took the opportunity to steal up behind me, and with his mouth grabbed my new hat....[W]hen I saw the danger my poor hat was in, I confess to the weakness of bringing my prayer to an abrupt close. I made at the colt, who, refusing to drop my hat, ran off to the woods, and I after him.

—John Dixon Long, *Pictures of Slavery in Church and State*, 1857

Samuel Green, a free colored man of Dorchester County, Maryland, was sentenced to ten years' confinement in the Maryland State prison, at the spring term of the County Court of the present year 1857, held in Cambridge, Md. What was the crime imputed to this man, born on American soil—a man of good moral character—a local preacher in the M.E. Church, as I have been informed—a husband and a father? Simply this—a copy of "Uncle Tom's Cabin" was found in his possession....He had recently paid a visit to his son residing in Canada. Previous to his arrest, several slaves had escaped to the land of the free.

—John Dixon Long, *Pictures of Slavery in Church and State*, 1857

ABOVE: Reverend Samuel Green (from William Still, "Samuel Green Alias Wesley Kinnard, August 28, 1854") depicts the East New Market pastor sentenced to ten years of prison—in part from association with his son Samuel's flight to Canada. *From* The Underground Rail Road, *1872.*

OPPOSITE: Lane Methodist Episcopal Church, built in 1897, replaced an earlier "coloured church" built around the time of the Civil War next to Bethlehem Methodist Episcopal Church. Bethlehem Church recognized "Barzillia [Basil?] Lane, Col'd" as an exhorter (a layman licensed to preach and evangelize), "examined and recommended to preach." The original church is documented in its location next to Bethlehem Church as seen in Martenet's *Atlas* of 1865 and the Lake, Griffing & Stevenson *Illustrated Atlas* of 1877. *Charlie Ewers.*

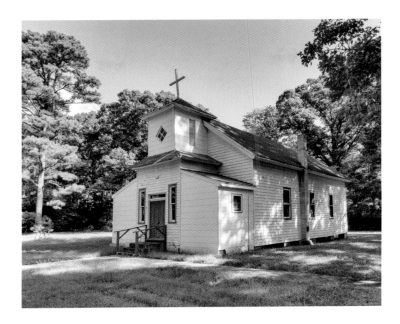

The original colored churches in different sections of the country came about in one of the following ways:

1. They were in some cases the result of special missionary effort on the part of the whites.

2. They were brought about by direct discrimination against the blacks made by the whites during divine worship.

3. They were the natural sequence, when, on account of increase in members, it became necessary for congregations to divide, whereupon the blacks were evolved as distinct churches, but still under the oversight, if not the exclusive control, of the whites.

4. They were, in not a few cases, the preference of colored communicants themselves, in order to get as much as possible the equal privileges and advantages of government denied them under the existing system.

—John W. Cromwell, "The Earlier Churches and Preachers," in W.E.B. Du Bois, *The Negro Church*, 1903

[Samuel Green] was an old local preacher in the Methodist Church—much esteemed as an inoffensive, industrious man; earning his bread by the sweat of his brow, and contriving to move along in the narrow road allotted colored people bond or free, without exciting a spirit of ill will in the proslavery power of his community. But the rancor awakened in the breast of slave-holders in consequence of the high-handed step the son had taken, brought the father under suspicion and hate....

To his utter consternation, not long after his return from his visit to his son "a party of gentlemen from the New Market district, went at night to Green's house and made search, whereupon was found a copy of Uncle Tom's Cabin, etc." This was enough—the hour had come, wherein to wreak vengeance upon poor Green....

In the case of the State against Sam Green, (free negro) who was tried at the April term of the Circuit Court of this county, for having in his possession abolition pamphlets, among which was "Uncle Tom's Cabin," has been found guilty by the court, and sentenced to the penitentiary for the term of ten years.

—William Still, "Samuel Green Alias Wesley Kinnard, August 28, 1854," *The Underground Rail Road*, 1872

The [Black congregation in the gallery] fired up immediately. There was [African American Reverend Richard] "Uncle Dick" Parker, in those days, who was not very far behind the Elder himself in effective appeal. The fire began to burn.... The cold and comfortless white people listened until they forgot their dismal surroundings, joining in the happy choruses started in the gallery and shouting as fervently after awhile as the others. In the excitement which ensued, Dr. Sammy Melson was on his feet, walking the aisles, waving his hands, and helping in the hallelujah.

With big tears coming down his cheeks, he turned to the pulpit, saying, "Brother White, these colored people have the spirit of the Lord among them, while we are as cold as an icicle."

—Adam Wallace (ed. by Joseph F. di Paolo), *My Business Was to Fight the Devil*, 1998

ABOVE: Carter N. Berkeley, "Virginia—Scene of a Colored Revival Meeting." This image may give us an idea of the impact of "Uncle Dick" Parker's preaching and how it warmed up the Salisbury congregation—Black and white worshippers alike—on a cold winter morning. *From* Frank Leslie's Illustrated Newspaper, September 12, 1885.

Right there nearly forty years ago I attended a great church dedication in the county town of Dorchester, Md....All the clergy stayed that night at Rev. Dr. Thompson's house. Rev. Dr. Thompson was a first-class physician, a human Christian slave-holder [emphasis added] and a fine preacher. About Midnight perhaps, there was a great "cry made" in the direction of "the quarter," where the slaves stayed. Some of the ministers, indeed all of us, thought that some atrocious deed had been done, and some person perhaps was murdered, but this fear and trembling was only for a short period. We heard them singing after wrestling with God in prayer and I shall never forget the song:

"Oh He died for you and he died for me.
He died to set poor sinners free."

∽

We listened attentively, and heard the words, "Hallelujah! Glory!! Glory !!!" It was the power of God amongst the Doctor's coloured people in the Quarter, a short distance from where we were lodging. "At midnight they prayed and sang praises unto God, and we heard them." Our fears were allayed, and we were led to cry out while we listened to their shouts:

"In every land begin the song,
To every land the strains belong,
In cheerful songs all voices raise,
And fill the world with sounding praise."

Two accounts of the same incident by Andrew Manship, describing praying from the slave quarters at the estate of Dr. Anthony Thompson, on whose property Harriet Tubman lived with other family members hired away from Edward Brodess. First section from the *Philadelphia Inquirer*, "In Slavery Days," February 22, 1891; second section from *Thirteen Years in the Itinerancy*, 1857.

The New Revived United Methodist Church (formerly the Jefferson Memorial Methodist Episcopal Church), Smithville. Built in 1924 (relocating a nearby congregation that went back to 1876), this church and adjoining school served an African American community of farmers, woodchoppers and watermen. As chronicled in *Smithville*, the Maryland Sea Grant film directed by Wyman Jones and produced and written by Rona Kobell, the congregation now faces flooding of its cemetery from the advancing marsh. Stressing the need to address the losses that come from communities whose churches and cemeteries are disappearing with rising sea levels, Dr. Sacoby Wilson of the University of Maryland College Park School of Public Health noted, "The environmental justice movement is not just about fighting hazards, but it is about protecting culture." *Charlie Ewers.*

As she recovered from this long illness, a deeper religious spirit seemed to take possession of her than she had ever experienced before. She literally "prayed without ceasing." "Pears like, I prayed all de time," she said, "about my work, eberywhere; I was always talking to de Lord. When I went to the horse-trough to wash my face, and took up de water in my hands, I said, 'Oh, Lord, wash me, make me clean.' When I took up de towel to wipe my face and hands, I cried, 'Oh, Lord, for Jesus' sake, wipe away all my sins!' When I took up de broom and began to sweep, I groaned, 'Oh, Lord, whatsoebber sin dere be in my heart, sweep it out, Lord, clar and clean.'"

—Sarah Hopkins Bradford, *Harriet, the Moses of Her People*, 1886

I was then between ten and eleven years old, and I continued to look for Him until I began to feel very sorry that He would not come and talk with me; and then I felt that I was the worst little boy that ever lived, and that was the reason Jesus would not talk to me....At last, I gave myself up to the Lord, to do what he would with me, for I was a great sinner....In the midst of my troubles, I felt that if God would have mercy on me, I should never sin again. When I had come to this, I felt my guilt give way, and thought that I was a new being.

—Peter Randolph, *Sketches of Slave Life*, 1855

⚬

After [his servant took] *Naaman into the water for his first bath,* [the Reverend Frost Pollet] *represented him as saying: "I don't b'lieve in dis heah nonsense, an' I'se a gwine ter come out'n dis ole ditch." Frost represented, in most dramatic language and manner, Naaman's successive baths...."And—he—went—down—the—seventh —time...!" "An' he come up out'n de water, an' his flesh was jest like a sweet, little baby's!"*

—Robert W. Todd, *Methodism of the Peninsula*, 1886

The story of Naaman the Aramean was a common subject for sermons and may have influenced Harriet Tubman's prayer to be washed clean.

GARY L. MOORE

The people who came to Trinity/New Hughes Church wanted to be there. It was near where they worked. It was a shelter from a hard life. It was where they worshipped with other Methodists.

When you worshipped here, you didn't worry about whether you were Black or white. You were focused on the preacher and responded to him or her. That preaching went to everybody in the congregation. It was a distinctive religious experience. You shouted if you were Black or white.

Originally, Methodists may have worshipped under a tree. They might gather outdoors, in barns, in carriage houses, in their homes—wherever they could meet. They wanted to be together. They were exuberant in a new religion.

Although the first Methodists of Dorchester County met not far from here in Aireys in the home of a wealthy landowner, most early Methodists were Black and white small farmers and laborers. They worked together. They met when they could—not always on a Sunday. It was "come as you are." It was wherever you could worship. It was for anybody who wanted to come.

The people focused on the spiritual aspects of life, not on building institutions. That was Methodism's appeal. It welcomed emotion as a connection to God and had practices for doing this. The message was that wherever they were, God was there. In good English or bad, you could express yourself through your emotion.

They formed classes that encouraged soulful introspection. Those who had the talent would lead. Anyone could attain this leadership. It didn't make a difference if you went to school or if you had accumulated wealth. In the case of Black Methodists it was not about

Charlie Ewers.

work. It was not about being abused. It was about being lifted up and accepting your dignity.

They all shared the worry about their spiritual destiny. They knew that they would die soon. They needed to know where they stood with God. They desired to be accepted by God—even if they were sinners. This religious experience enabled Black Methodists to question their worldly experience. They may have been enslaved, but they had hope. They would go to worship with their white brothers and sisters and then would continue their worship after the others had left.

By the time of the Dorchester days of Harriet Tubman, worship had brought Black and white Methodists together for forty years. It provided the freedom of their own religious experience. It allowed them to be who they were.

In the case of Black worshippers, church people learned how to lead small groups and worship services. The church approved local lay pastors and ordained local Black ministers. These ministers gave examples of Black leadership and taught the dignity of Black expression.

At the same time, white Methodists were doing well. They became middle class. Congregations and churches became larger. They felt diminishing emotional experience in church. The Methodist Episcopal Church began to break apart into the Methodist Protestant Church and the Methodist Episcopal Church South. By the 1840s, Black Christians began to have their own services within the larger Methodist system of shared ministry.

Beyond the background of slavery and the economic system it promoted, Harriet Tubman's story was of faith through her Methodism. She inherited this faith. She experienced it in her day-to-day life. It led her to understand that in God's eyes she was free.

She had come to the biblical understanding that we share our lives with Jesus. This faith was not only personal, but also plain for anyone to see. She expressed this in her entire life. Her faith deserves acceptance for what it was. It was not narrowed by her circumstances, but rather broadened by the message she learned at birth and shared throughout her life.

—REVEREND GARY L. MOORE,
Retired, the United Methodist Church, Easton, Maryland

8

Blessed of My Father

TALKING WITH GOD AND SEEING VISIONS

Once known as the Bucktown Mission Methodist Episcopal Church, Bazel's Chapel (also spelled Bazzle and Bazzel) dates back at least to the 1876 date on its cornerstone and to 1877, when it appeared on the Lake, Griffing & Stevenson *Illustrated Atlas of Talbot & Dorchester Counties, Maryland*. The current chapel building dates from 1911. Located in the center of a community of African American laborers and farmers that flourished in the nineteenth century, the site—no longer an active church—is associated with Harriet Tubman's relatives and was opened for annual commemorative services in honor of Harriet Tubman in the twentieth century. *Charlie Ewers*.

Brought up by parents possessed of strong faith in God, she had never known the time, I imagine, when she did not trust Him, and cling to Him, with an all-abiding confidence.

—Sarah Hopkins Bradford, *Harriet, the Moses of Her People*, 1886

TOP: Frank Vizetelly, "Family Worship in a Plantation in South Carolina." This image reveals much about African American worship. It shows the fervor of the preacher/exhorter as he addresses the group. The title of the image testifies to the "venerable patriarch" (as described by W.E.B. Du Bois) as the leader of a family group of worshippers and, eventually, a church. Finally, it shows a white minister or deacon sitting in on the worship, a practice that became more widespread after Nat Turner's Rebellion. *From* The Illustrated London News, *December 5, 1863.*

BOTTOM: Jack Delano, "Siloam, Greene County, Georgia, Singing class in a Negro School, 1941." Perhaps reflecting what James W. Alexander, *Thoughts on Family-worship*, believed "to be most like the praise of God" in sacred music, the members of this singing class impressed the photographer with their fervor. *Library of Congress.*

[Harriet Tubman's parents] come in every Sunday—more than a mile—to the Central Church. To be sure, deep slumbers settle down upon them as soon as they are seated, which continue undisturbed till the congregation is dismissed; but they have done their best, and who can doubt that they receive a blessing. Immediately after this they go to class-meeting at the Methodist Church. Then they wait for a third service, and after that start out home again.

On asking Harriet where they got anything to eat on Sunday, she said, in her quiet way, "Oh! de ole folks nebber eats anyting on Sunday, Missis! We nebber has no food to get for dem on Sunday. Dey always fasts; and dey nebber eats anyting on Fridays. Good Friday, an' five Fridays hand gwine from Good Friday, my fader nebber eats or drinks, all day—fasting for de five bleeding wounds ob Jesus. All the oder Fridays ob de year he nebber eats till de sun goes down; den he takes a little tea an' a piece ob bread." "But is he a Roman Catholic, Harriet?" "Oh no, Misses; he does it for conscience; we was taught to do so down South. He says if he denies himself for the sufferings of his Lord an' Master, Jesus will sustain him."

—Sarah Hopkins Bradford, *Scenes in the Life of Harriet Tubman*, 1869

⁂

Very early in life [Sarah Jane Woodson Early] showed a disposition to learn whatever came within her reach. At the age of three she could sing all the hymns used at family worship. At five she could commit large portions of the Bible to memory.

—Monroe Alphus Majors, "Mrs. S.J.W. Early," in *Noted Negro Women*, 1893

As with many men and women in the faith, Harriet Tubman demonstrated a thorough knowledge of hymns and the Bible, acquired through her worship with family and with congregations.

The fondness of the black race for music is proverbial. It is rare to meet with a negro who does not sing; and there are many whose organ is susceptible of extraordinary training. It is not uncommon to hear the negro, on some nightly walk through the forest, waking the echoes with a sacred song, and perhaps, (odd as it may seem), giving out the lines to himself. We have listened to a great variety of sacred music, vocal and instrumental...in choirs and congregations, in concerts and oratorios; but if we were summoned to declare which of all seemed most like the praise of God, we should reply, The united voices of a thousand slaves, ascending to heaven in a volume of harmony.

—James W. Alexander, *Thoughts on Family-worship*, 1847

How exciting it was to hear her tell the story. And to hear the very scraps of jubilant hymns that [Josiah "Joe" Bailey, in flight from slave-catchers, arriving in Canada] sang.

—Charlotte Forten Grimké, diary, 1863

[Harriet Tubman] told stories, sang songs, danced, and imitated the talk of the Southern Negroes.

—Sarah Hopkins Bradford, *Harriet, the Moses of Her People*, 1901

In her own home, Harriet delights to welcome any who may come, opening her treasury of story and song for their benefit.

—Emma Paddock Telford, *Harriet: The Modern Moses of Heroism and Visions*, circa 1905

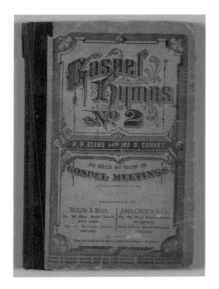

LEFT: This copy of *Gospel Hymns No. 2* by P.P. Bliss and Ira D. Sankey was Harriet Tubman's personal hymnal. Given Harriet Tubman's knowledge of hymns, one wonders whether this book may have been a gift that she perhaps shared with her visitors who might not know all the hymns sung at a service. *The Smithsonian National Museum of African American History and Culture, Gift of Charles L. Blockson.*

BELOW: William Ludwell Sheppard, "The sunny South—A negro revival meeting—a seeker 'getting religion,'" *Frank Leslie's illustrated Newspaper*, Library of Congress, August 1873. Reading the image beyond the title and Sheppard's outsider perspective, one can imagine the mutual support and comfort stemming from a Methodist prayer service or class meeting.

The Hymn-Book is the colored people's only catechism. Many of them could state the cardinal doctrines of the Gospel in the language of song. I have been conversant with their class-meetings for years, and am familiar with their peculiar manner and language in the relation of their experience....

The name of John Gladding is called. John arises, and the leader thus addresses him: "Tell your class how you are prospering in religion." John.–"My brothers and sisters, I had a great desire to come here to tell you how I have been getting along in religion, in the past week. I tell you, brothers, that religion is good all the time, 'long the fence-roads as well as in the church. I feel Jesus in my soul. I am bound for the kingdom. Pray for me that I may hold out, and hold on, and get to heaven when I die." "Amen!" says one; "Glory!" ejaculates another. Leader.–"Watch and pray, John; he that endureth to the end shall be saved." A sweet hymn is sung:

A charge to keep I have,
A God to glorify;
A never-dying soul to save,
And fit it for the sky....

—John Dixon Long, *Pictures of Slavery in Church and State*, 1857
Charles Wesley, "A Charge to Keep I Have," 1762

But she must first give some intimation of her purpose
to the friends she was to leave behind, so that even if not
understood at the time, it might be remembered afterward
as her intended farewell. Slaves must not be seen talking
together, and so it came about that their communication
was often made by singing, and the words of their familiar
hymns, telling of the heavenly journey, and the land of
Canaan, while they did not attract the attention of the
masters, conveyed to their brethren and sisters in bondage
something more than met the ear. And so she sang,
accompanying the words, when for a moment unwatched,
with a meaning look to one and another:

When dat ar ole chariot comes,
I'm gwine to lebe you,
I'm boun' for de promised land,
Frien's, I'm gwine to lebe you.

Again, as she passed the doors of the different cabins,
she lifted up her well-known voice; and many a dusky face
appeared at door or window, with a wondering or scared
expression; and thus she continued:

I'm sorry, frien's, to lebe you,
Farewell! oh, farewell!
But I'll meet you in de mornin',
Farewell! oh, farewell!

I'll meet you in de mornin',
When you reach de promised land;
On de oder side of Jordan,
For I'm boun' for de promised land.

—Sarah Hopkins Bradford, *Harriet, the Moses of Her People*, 1886

FAREWELL, dear friends, I must be gone,
I have no home or stay with you;
I'll take my staff and travel on,
Till I a better country view.
I'll march to Canaan's land,
I'll land on Canaan's shore;
Where pleasures never end.
Where troubles come no more.
Farewell, farewell, farewell,
My loving friends, farewell.

—Samuel Crossman, "Hymn 265, L.M., Farewell, Dear Friends," *Hymns Designed
for Protracted, Camp, Prayer and Social Meetings*, 1852

ABOVE: The song sung by Harriet Tubman when she left her native land may have been
inspired by the farewell hymns of the camp meetings, such as Carey's Camp, still held each
year in Millsboro, Delaware. Adam Wallace, *Parson of the Islands*, 1872, offers a vivid image
of one of these camp meetings on Deal's Island in 1838, describing "permanent tents on the
front rows, reaching entirely round the circle....The second, third, and sometimes the fourth
and fifth rows were occupied by persons from the main and distant islands....Away towards
the eastward, the colored people encamped, and held at intervals their lively exercises."
Charlie Ewers.

I'm sorry I'm gwine to lebe you,
Farewell, oh farewell;
But I'll meet you in the mornin',
Farewell, oh farewell.

I'll meet you in the mornin',
I'm boun' for de promised land,
On the oder side of Jordan,
Boun' for de promised land.

I'll meet you in the mornin',
Safe in de promised land,
On the oder side of Jordan,
Boun' for de promised land.

An earlier improvisation of the "farewell" song (above) in Sarah Hopkins
Bradford, *Scenes in the Life of Harriet Tubman*, 1869

CAMP MEETING—The Steamboat
PAUL JONES, Capt. McNelty, will leave LIGHT ST.
WHARF, on SATURDAY, 1st August, at 8½ o'clock
P.M., for the CAMP MEETING at "Tobacco Stick," in
Dorchester county, and return the following evening, at
the same hour.

The steamboat will go within 100 yards of the
landing, and not more than 2 or 300 yards from the
Camp Ground.
Passage each way, $1.
N.B. There will be no Bar on board. Breakfast will be
served on board if requested.

(Baltimore) *Sun*, "Camp Meeting," July 30, 1840. It is possible that Harriet
Tubman attended this camp meeting in Tobacco Stick, now Madison.

[Camp meetings] are generally held in the summer time—in some central position, on an elevated spot, shaded with beautiful oak and hickory trees, and where water can easily be obtained. The camp consists of a circle of tents, numbering from fifty to three hundred, made of plank or canvas. The space included within the first circle of tents, excepting the avenue for walking or promenading, is consecrated to religious worship. Within this inclosure a rough and substantial pulpit is erected, immediately in front of which is a place denominated the altar, where those who seek the forgiveness of their sins come forward to be prayed for. Still further on are seats for the white congregation. Behind the pulpit, and separated by a board fence, is the place allotted for the colored people, who labor under the disadvantage of not catching the inspiration which darts from the eye of an earnest orator, or beams from a countenance irradiated by heavenly enthusiasm....

Scenes which can never be blotted from my memory: Campfires blazing in every direction with heart pine wood; the groans and the sobs of penitent sinners; the shout and the rapture of the new convert; the rejoicing of friends; the deep, melodious, organ-like music welling from a thousand African throats—all conspired to elevate the soul to Christ, "who sitteth at the right hand of the Father."

—John Dixon Long, *Pictures of Slavery in Church and State*, 1857

RIGHT: A few of the modern "tents" of Carey's Camp in Millsboro, Delaware. *Charlie Ewers.*

In the old-time Peninsula camp-meetings, the colored people were always provided for; a portion of the circle to the rear of the preacher's stand being invariably set apart for their occupancy and use. Here they drew up their covered carts, and erected their nondescript tents. The latter often consisted of poles stuck into the earth, and bent and tied together; over which they spread such articles of bed-clothing as they might happen to possess, to afford the needed shelter. Not infrequently their tents were of patchwork, after the pattern of Joseph's coat, or a modern crazy-quilt; and added a ludicrous feature to the weird scenery of the primitive encampment.

In front of their tents, and generally in the most open and sunny spot obtainable, was their shouting-ground, or meeting-place; where, after the sermon, they were wont to gather for the great revival effort. This service was usually opened by the formal announcement of some solemn hymn, such as, "And am I born to die?" or, "Hark, from the tomb the doleful sound;" which was sung to a melancholy minor, in the slowest time possible, and slurred and tremoloed into all sorts of fantastic shapes...."Brudder Jacob Isr'el Potter," or "Isaier Ishm'el Carter," or some other recognized dignitary, was called on to "lead in de revotions at de throne ob grace."

ABOVE: Another view of Carey's Camp, Millsboro, Delaware. *Charlie Ewers.*

The space thus enclosed was devoted to penitents; and
there, kneeling on the bare ground—ofttimes prostrate in
the dust—many a wounded spirit, from the double bondage,
human and satanic, found the liberty of Christ and the "balm
in Gilead." Many of the most jubilant songs of the negroes
pointed with glowing metaphor to this blessed, spiritual
freedom, and to the coming good time when the Immortal
Liberator should break their last fetter. The following stanza
and chorus, heard a thousand times in my boyhood, will
serve as an illustration:

"O! sinner; run to Jesus;
Wid a mighty hand he frees us;
An' ole Satin neber tease us,
Ef de Lord do appear.
Chorus: Den you will git free
In de year ob jubilee;
Yes, childring, we'll be free
When de Lord do appear...!"

Usually the tide of enthusiasm, on the colored side of the
encampment, arose and intensified as the days and nights
rolled by; and reached the climactic point on the last night
of the meeting. By general consent, it was understood that,
as to the colored people, the rules requiring quiet after a
certain hour, were, on this last night, to be suspended; and
great billows of sound from the tornado of praise and singing
rolled over the encampment, and was echoed back from hill
and wood for miles away, until the morrow's dawning.

To those in the tents, this hour was usually signaled by
the sound of hammer and axe, knocking down the plank
partition walls separating the white and colored precincts;
and, in a few moments, the grand "march 'round de'
campment" was inaugurated, accompanied with leaping,
shuffling, and dancing, after the order of David before the
ark when his wife thought he was crazy; accompanied by a
song appropriate to the exciting occasion. Some of my readers
will recognize the following couplets:

"We's a marchin' away to Canaann's land;
I hears de music ob de angel band.
Chorus—"O come an' jine de army;
An' we'll keep de ark a movin';

"As we goes shoutin' home!
Come, childering, storm ole Jericho's walls;
Yes, blow an' shout, an' down dey falls!"
Chorus—"O come," etc....

The sound of the hammer aforesaid became the signal for a general arising all around the camp; and, in a few moments, curtains were parted; tents thrown open; and multitudes of faces peered out into the early dawning to witness the weird spectacle. Sometimes the voices of the masters and veterans among the white people would echo back, in happy response, the jubilant shout of the rejoicing slaves.

—Robert W. Todd, *Methodism of the Peninsula*, 1880

While in Canada, in 1860, we met several whom [Harriet Tubman] *had brought from the land of bondage, and they all believed that she had supernatural power. Of one man we inquired, "Were you not afraid of being caught?"*

"O, no," said he, "Moses is got de charm."

"What do you mean?' we asked.

He replied, "De whites can't catch Moses, kase you see she's born wid de charm. De Lord has given Moses de power."

Yes, and the woman herself felt that she had the charm, and this feeling, no doubt, nerved her up, gave her courage, and made all who followed her feel safe in her hands.

—William Wells Brown, *The Rising Sun*, 1874

I heard they said she was a conjure. That's what they used to put on the people in those days when they was doin' things.

—Nicey Ross Ennals, in Hal Roth, *Two Pieces of Clothes*, 2003

ABOVE: J.C. Darby, "Harriet, in her costume as scout," in Sarah Hopkins Bradford. In her Civil War garb, Harriet Tubman would have carried herbal medicines in her bag to treat the soldiers and others under her care. *From* Scenes in the Life of Harriet Tubman, *1869.*

To this day, many ignorant whites, and perhaps one-half the colored population of the Peninsula, have as much faith in witches and ghosts as they have in the existence of a Great First Cause; and, by charms and exorcisms, take more pains to propitiate the goblins than they do to secure the favor of their Redeemer. To correct these superstitions is the work of the churches and the schools.

—Robert W. Todd, *Methodism of the Peninsula*, 1880

Robert Todd's faith and his prejudice against African American and white people of Delmarva both are on display here.

They believe in second-sight, in apparitions, charms, witchcraft, and in a kind of irresistible Satanic influence. The superstitions brought from Africa have not been wholly laid aside....On certain occasions they have been made to believe that while they carried about their persons some charm with which they had been furnished, they were *invulnerable*. They have, on certain other occasions, been made to believe that they were under a protection that rendered them *invincible*. That they might go any where and do any thing they pleased, and it would be impossible for them to be discovered or known; in fine, to will was to do—safely, successfully.

—Charles C. Jones, *The Religious Instruction of Negroes in the United States*, 1842

[Sandy] *was not only a religious man, but he professed to believe in a system for which I have no name. He was a genuine African, and had inherited some of the so-called magical powers....He told me that he could help me; that in those very woods there was an herb...possessing all the powers required for my protection...and that if I would take his advice he would procure me the root of the herb of which he spoke. He told me, further, that if I would take that root and wear it on my right side it would be impossible for Covey to strike me a blow; that with this root about my person no white man could whip me....*

Now all this talk about the root was to me very absurd and ridiculous, if not positively sinful. I at first rejected the idea...."My book-learning" he said, "had not kept Covey off me" (a powerful argument just then), and he entreated me, with flashing eyes, to try this. If it did me no good it could do me no harm, and it would cost me nothing any way. Sandy was so earnest and so confident of the good qualities of this weed that, to please him, I was induced to take it....

Just as I entered the yard gate I met him [Covey] and his wife, dressed in their Sunday best, looking as smiling as angels, on their way to church. His manner perfectly astonished me.... This extraordinary conduct really made me begin to think that Sandy's herb had more virtue in it than I, in my pride, had been willing to allow, and had the day been other than Sunday I should have attributed Covey's altered manner solely to the power of the root. I suspected, however, that the Sabbath, not the root, was the real explanation of the change.

—Frederick Douglass, *Life and Times of Frederick Douglass*, 1881

Then she says she always knows when there is danger near her—she does not know how, exactly, but "'pears like my heart go flutter, flutter, and den dey may say 'Peace, Peace,' as much as dey likes, I know its gwine to be war." She is very firm on this point, and ascribes to this her great impunity, in spite of the lethargy before mentioned, which would seem likely to throw her into the hands of her enemies. She says she inherited this power, that her father could always predict the weather, and that he foretold the Mexican war.

—Franklin B. Sanborn, "Harriet Tubman," the (Boston) *Commonwealth*, July 17, 1863

[On] the plantation she was prone to strange dreams which came to her suddenly while working or while conversing with her fellow slaves. In one of these she saw a ship's deck with black men in murderous revolt and white men lying with crimson stains upon the flooring. In another she was on a ship at night and a Negro woman, clasping a child to her bosom, crept from below and leaped into the sea. The old mammies to whom she told these dreams were wont to nod knowingly and say, "I reckon youse one o' dem 'Shantees', chile." For they knew the tradition of the unconquerable Ashantee blood....At this time Harriet began to develop a wonderful gift of prescience and abnormal cunning, so that many of her dreams soon or later came startlingly true.

—Frank C. Drake, "The Moses of Her People," *New York Herald*, 1907

TOP: "Africans Thrown Overboard from a Slave Ship, Brazil" or "Extract from a Letter Dated Rio de Janeiro." The content of Harriet Tubman's "strange dreams" may only be hinted at from this illustration of the *Zong* Massacre from William Lloyd Garrison's newspaper. *From* The Liberator, *January 1832.*

BOTTOM: Thomas Nast, "Contrabands Coming into our Lines Under the Proclamation." Harriet Tubman's vision of her people being free, described to Reverend Henry Highland Garnet, was to be realized in a few more years. *From* Harper's Weekly, *May 9, 1863.*

While staying with the Rev. Henry Highland Garnet in New York, a vision came to her in the night of the emancipation of her people. Whether a dream, or one of those glimpses into the future, which sometimes seem to have been granted to her, no one can say, but the effect upon her was very remarkable.

She rose singing, "My people are free!" "My people are free!" She came down to breakfast singing the words in a sort of ecstasy. She could not eat. The dream or vision filled her whole soul, and physical needs were forgotten.

Mr. Garnet said to her:

"Oh, Harriet! Harriet! You've come to torment us before the time; do cease this noise! My grandchildren may see the day of the emancipation of our people, but you and I will never see it."

"I tell you, sir, you'll see it, and you'll see it soon. My people are free! My people are free."

—Sarah Hopkins Bradford, *Harriet, the Moses of Her People*, 1886

At one time she was called away from Hilton Head, by one of our officers, to come to Fernandina, where the men were "dying off like sheep," from dysentery. Harriet had acquired quite a reputation for her skill in curing this disease, by a medicine which she prepared from roots which grew near the waters which gave the disease. Here she found thousands of sick soldiers and contrabands, and immediately gave up her time and attention to them. At another time, we find her nursing those who were down by hundreds with small-pox and malignant fevers. She had never had these diseases, but she seems to have no more fear of death in one form than another. "De Lord would take keer of her till her time came, an' den she was ready to go."

—Sarah Hopkins Bradford, *Scenes in the Life of Harriet Tubman*, 1869

In the hospital camps she would nurse a case of scarlet fever or small-pox with as much indifference to contagion as if it were chicken pox or stomach ache. For the latter, she had a sovereign remedy, a one-day "yarb" cure, especially effective for dysentery. All her postwar life, she made trips to whatever woodland was adjacent, for the purpose of digging the root that was the basis of her remedy. The identity of the plant was her well-kept secret.

—Samuel Hopkins Adams, *Grandfather Stories*, 1947

ABOVE: "Dewberry, Rubus Flagellaris." This plant may be one of the "yarbs" used by Harriet Tubman to nurse soldiers in the Civil War, treating dysentery with a solution made from the root. *Missouri Department of Conservation.*

Harriet's ability as an actress has been alluded to. One of her masterly accomplishments in this line, young as she was, was the impersonation of an old woman....[S]he had the incredible nerve to enter a village where lived one of her former masters....Her only disguise was a bodily assumption of age.

—Frank C. Drake, "The Moses of Her People," *New York Herald*, 1907

Harriet herself assuming her favorite guise of a tottering old woman, stood at the foot of the commissioner's stairs.... The officers were bringing the Negro down the stairs to the wagon....Harriet, throwing off her disguise, shouted: "Here he is! Here he is! Take him!"

With these words, she pounced upon the marshal with all her gigantic strength and bore him to the ground. Then...she seized the prisoner and with the mad ferocity of her ancestors fought her way down the street.

—Frank C. Drake, "The Moses of Her People," *New York Herald*, 1907

With a daring almost heedless, she went even to the very village where she would be most likely to meet one of the masters to whom she had been hired; and having stopped at the Market and bought a pair of live fowls, she went along the street with her sun-bonnet well over her face, and with the bent and decrepit air of an aged woman.

—Sarah Hopkins Bradford, *Harriet, the Moses of Her People*, 1886

I hardly know how to approach the subject of the spiritual experiences of my sable heroine. They seem so to enter into the realm of the supernatural, that I can hardly wonder that those who never knew her are ready to throw discredit upon the story. Ridicule has been cast upon the whole tale of her adventures by the advocates of human slavery; and perhaps by those who would tell with awe-struck countenance some tale of ghostly visitation, or spiritual manifestation, at a dimly lighted "seance."

Had I not known so well her deeply religious character, and her conscientious veracity, and had I not since the war, and when she was an inmate of my own house, seen such remarkable instances of what seemed to be her direct intercourse with heaven, I should not dare to risk my own character for veracity by making these things public in this manner.

—Sarah Hopkins Bradford, *Harriet, the Moses of Her People,* 1897

ABOVE: "Another Trying to Down Her, She Choked into Half Unconsciousness," Frank C. Drake, "The Moses of Her People." Harriet Tubman in disguise as a "tottering old woman" freeing Charles Nalle. *From* New York Herald, *September 22, 1907.*

For in truth I never met with any person,
of any color, who had more confidence
in the voice of God, as spoken direct to
her soul. She has frequently told me that
she talked with God, and he talked with
her every day of her life, and she has
declared to me that she felt no more fear
of being arrested by her former master, or
any other person, when in his immediate
neighborhood, than she did in the State
of New York, or Canada, for she said she
never ventured only where God sent her,
and her faith in the Supreme Power truly
was great.

—Thomas Garrett, in Sarah Hopkins Bradford, *Harriet, the Moses of Her People*, 1897

SHIRLYN HENRY BROWN

When I think of Bazel's Chapel, I see wooden benches. I smell burning wood in the stove. I hear the prayer band singing, lifted by the Holy Ghost. I think of the children saying their prayers in Sunday school. The pastor preaching grace. An all-day service of worship and people sharing a meal. A small, but mighty, place to find peace.

Charlie Ewers.

Before Bazel's Chapel was built, people would say, "Let's go down to the river," to the bush—to a spiritual building. In this sacred place, they would find solace in the bush. The Holy Ghost lifting voice and praise. The preacher praying and singing, "Come Holy Spirit, give us peace." They would lay their burdens down. It was their time of rest, where they could feel free and not be bound by what they have to walk back to.

When Harriet Tubman lived in Bucktown, she had a large family of faith who joined her at worship. After all, who defines family? We are brothers and sisters who come together. We will see each other through what happens. A grandmother will rock a child of six. She is not a biological parent, but a mother of the church.

Harriet Tubman's knowing both of her parents was a privilege and a blessing. Members of her family could worship together on Sunday. The church was an anchor and a foundation of her birth family. You become a founding family in the congregation. The faith of her father became her faith. Her father's God became her God. This happened because she was born to it. The faith of Harriet Tubman was a vital part of what she was. She wanted to keep families together through the Underground Railroad. It was a life she lived because family was part of her.

Hymns and songs were a way of communicating. Many could not read, but they could sing. The lyrics are the story. You can communicate through song. They might be telling you a story to start your escape, going that night. On the other hand, the hymn "I want Jesus to walk with me" is the story of the burdens of everyday life, its trials, its sorrows, its troubles.

They knew the Bible stories—Moses and the escape of the Hebrews. There will be trouble, but it won't last always. People would sing "Steal Away," knowing that they haven't long to be on this Earth. They would sing "Give Me Jesus." These hymns became their faith, their source of wisdom—their teacher, their educator. They might not always get that knowledge from a sermon, but they would get it from song. They would always get it. The word becomes "are you listening?"

My great-grandmother could not read. She was the daughter of a freedman, but she could quote scripture and hymns. She went to church every Sunday. I once told a speech student, "Do you know it not by memory, but by heart?" In a nursing home, my great-grandmother knew it by heart. Harriet Tubman's family went to church, so she knew everything by heart. At the age of six, Harriet Tubman was like a sponge. She soaked up everything.

Harriet Tubman found justifying grace in her time: "I knew God myself," she said. "I acknowledged him as my savior. In him, I can do anything. My visions acknowledge that I cannot do this without God." You recognize this is different. It is peace beyond understanding.

Yes, Harriet Tubman talked with God. Don't we all have communion with God? Doesn't Alice Walker in *The Color Purple* have Celie writing to God? Isn't that what prayers are? Prayer is a conversation with God. Harriet Tubman found peace because she knew who could make change.

My great-grandfather was a local preacher. Your life working in a house or in the field was a different life (from your life on Sunday), but you were one and the same person. In church, you could be there in authority—the deacon of a mother of the church. It was not only spiritual power but also your standing. You were trusted by the people in church. Harriet Tubman came from one of these families. You trusted that family. That trust even leveled the boundaries beyond church.

Why do we know so little about Harriet Tubman's faith? She tells her story orally. We tell her story as we have learned it, so it is a story of her conversations with God and what God worked through her—not what took place in a building. The church lived inside her. Harriet Tubman lived her faith. We can honor it as she lived it. It is not easy, but we can live it inside too.

—REVEREND DR. SHIRLYN HENRY BROWN
Pastor, Ezion–Mt. Carmel United Methodist Church
Former District Superintendent, Easton District,
Peninsula-Delaware Conference, United Methodist Church

9

A Long, Lonely Journey

CROSSING THE LINE AND APPLYING
TO THE RIGHT PEOPLE

Dorchester and other counties of the Delmarva Peninsula are crisscrossed by trails through woods and around marshes that linked bodies of water, settlements, roads and even railroads. Dating back to the Indians in many cases, these trails played a role in the flight of enslaved people from the slave-holding lands of "Egypt" to the free states of "Canaan" to the north. An alternative to roads or railroad tracks where those in flight might be exposed, trails provided a parallel route, a way to a protected "station" (a home of a sympathizer) on the Underground Railroad or a means of escape to a hiding place. A walking route such as this path in the Pemberton Historical Park in Wicomico County, Maryland, may give an idea of these pathways. *Charlie Ewers.*

When her master died, word went around the quarters that the slaves were to be "sold South," the thing most dreaded by negroes of the upper tier of Southern States.

—Charles Dennis, "The Work of Harriet Tubman," *Americana Magazine*, November 1911

❧

The surplus labour of the northern slave plantations finds a ready market in the Southern States, which have still so much unoccupied land.

—Robert Russell, *North America, Its Agriculture and Climate*, 1857

About two years and six months after my old master's death,
a division was made of the property. This involved a sale of
everything....There were, I believe, heavy debts hanging over the
estate....When it was made known in the kitchen that a sale
was to be made, the slaves were panic-stricken. Loud cries and
lamentations arose.

—Martha Griffith Browne, *Autobiography of a Female Slave*, 1857

OPPOSITE: The marina at Choptank, where workboats and pleasure boats begin their outings, is not far from where Harriet Tubman and her brothers began their first attempt at self-liberation. The current-day boat slips and fields are a far cry from the docks near the nineteenth-century timberlands where Ben Ross and his children worked. *Charlie Ewers.*

ABOVE, LEFT: J. Martenet, "Talbot County." *From* Martenet's Atlas of Maryland, *1865.*

ABOVE, RIGHT: *Harriet Tubman Underground Railroad Byway Driving Map, Site 24.*

One of my earliest recollections, when living in Cambridge, was the Georgia-man, or slave trader, who sat in a split-bottomed chair in the verandah of Bradshaw's Hotel, and sunned himself, and waited for propositions from slave owners. We boys feared him as a hobgoblin. I saw him every morning, on my way to school, in the opening of the year, for it was at this time that he made his annual northward journey for business purposes.

—John F. Hurst, in Robert W. Todd, *Methodism of the Peninsula*, 1880

TOP: "Slaves Being Sold in Public Auction," in Thomas L. Johnson, *Twenty-eight Years a Slave*, 1876, probably from Josiah Henson, *Uncle Tom's Story of His Life*, 1876. The illustration perhaps depicts "Georgia Traders" (*left*) attending the auction. *The Christian Age Publishers.*

BOTTOM: Wilson Armistead, "Husbands, Wives, and Families, Sold Indiscriminately to Different Purchasers Are Violently Separated—Probably Never to Meet Again," 1853. The scenes of the auction block, where people were so graphically treated as chattel, became emblematic of abolitionist art. *From Schomburg Center, New York Public Library.*

I remember one day seeing John, who was much older than the rest, with a small bundle in his hand, saying good-bye to his mother, while a white man stood waiting in the hall for him. His mother and mine, with others, were crying, and all seemed very sad. I did not know what to make of it. Some kind of fear came over me, but I did not know why. Soon we heard that the man who took John was the "Georgia Trader". All slave-traders were then called Georgia Traders. After this, whenever we saw a white man looking over the fence as we were at play, we would run and hide, sometimes getting near our mothers, thinking they could protect us.

—Thomas L. Johnson, *Twenty-eight Years a Slave*, 1876

☙

The separation of families seems to be an inevitable feature of slavery, as it exists at present. If a man is rich and benevolent, he will provide for his servants, and tax himself to support them, let their number be never so great, buying one plantation after another, chiefly to employ his people. But the time will come when he must die, and his people are deprived of his protection. No one child, perhaps, can afford to keep them together; perhaps he has no children; then they must take their chance of separations to the widest borders of the slave States.

—Nehemiah Adams, *A South-Side View of Slavery*, 1854

Despite his role of serving as an apologist for slavery, Adams concedes that family separation is inevitable in the system of slavery.

The first act of slavery which I recorded in my memory, was the sale of my elder sister....My mother heard of the sale, which was on Saturday, and on Sunday took us with her to see our beloved sister, who was then in the yard with the trader's drove, preparatory to being removed far south, on the Monday following.

As soon as my sister saw our mother, she ran to her and fell upon her neck, but was unable to speak a word. There was a scene which angels witnessed; there were tears which, I believe, were bottled and placed in God's depository, there to be reserved until the day when He shall pour His wrath upon this guilty nation.

The trader, becoming uneasy at this exciting scene, and fearing the rest of the drove would become dissatisfied with their situations, permitted sister to leave the yard for a few moments, to keep mother's company....[He] even permitted her to go about with mother, and even to accompany us part of our way towards home.

The time soon arrived when we must go. When mother was about to bid farewell to my sister, and reached out her hand to grasp hers, she burst into a flood of tears, exclaiming aloud, "Lord, have mercy upon me!"

The trader, seeing such parental affection, as he stood by, hung down his head and wiped the tears from his eyes; and to relieve himself from a scene so affecting, he said, "Mary, you can go some way with your mother, and return soon."

Turning to mother, he said, "Old woman, I will do the best I can for your daughter; I will sell her to a good master."

After going with us two miles, sister Mary, in obedience to orders and her promise, could go no farther, and she said, "Mother, I suppose I must go back."

Here another heart-rending scene took place. I well remember her parting words, "Mother," she said, "don't grieve, for though we are separated in body, our separation is only for a season, and if we are faithful we shall meet again where partings are no more."

—John Thompson, *Life of John Thompson, A Fugitive Slave*, 1856

She had already seen two older sisters taken away as part of a chain gang, and they had gone no one knew whither; she had seen the agonized expression on their faces as they turned to take a last look at their "Old Cabin Home;" and had watched them from the top of the fence, as they went off weeping and lamenting, till they were hidden from her sight forever.

—Harriet Hopkins Bradford, *Harriet, the Moses of Her People*, 1886

Men, women, and children, about forty in all, two by two, an ox chain passing through the double file, and a fastening reaching from the right and left hands of those on either side of the chain, composed what is called a slave coffle.

—Nehemiah Adams, *A South-Side View of Slavery*, 1855

ABOVE: Thomas Nast, "The Emancipation of the Negroes—The Past and the Future," *Harper's Weekly*, January 24, 1863, shows another image (*left*) of the slave auction. *Library of Congress*.

Harriet counselled the negroes to run away, but none had the courage to follow her. She knew only that if she followed the north star it would lead her to freedom, and one night she stole away. Of the terrible journey north she remembers little; her instinct guided her and her great strength enabled her to stand the privation.

"I had reasoned dis out in ma mind," she says. "Dere was one er two things I had er right to, liberty or death. Ef I couldn't hab one I'd hab de odder."

—Charles Dennis, "The Work of Harriet Tubman," *Americana Magazine,*
November 1911

ABOVE: The "Big Dipper" pointed to the North Star, "truly the slave's friend," in the words of William Wells Brown in his *Narrative* (1847), the principal signpost on the road north to freedom. *Charlie Ewers.*

OPPOSITE: This modern mosaic of photos of the Delmarva Peninsula from Landsat shows the Choptank, Nanticoke and other rivers pointing to the northeast to Philadelphia and freedom. Goddard Space Flight Center, "Beautiful New Landsat Mosaic of Chesapeake Bay" (detail), 2011. *Wikimedia Commons.*

[Harriet Tubman] went back, and sought concealment in the house of a friend who had first advised her escape. She made her arrival known to her friends, & her purpose, which was "to lead them out of Egypt." She had four brothers, two sisters, and their children, then slaves, to her old mistress.

—Sydney Howard Gay, *Journal*, 1855–56

The spring following, she returned a third time. Her four brothers had been fugitives all winter, in the woods, to escape the dreaded "chain gang." The three eldest, however, had "come in" at the solicitation of a lumber-man, to whom their services were important, & who had hired them before, and who had agreed to hire them again for one year, thus securing them from being sold before the next Christmas. The youngest, however, was not included in this arrangement, & remained in the woods, tho' badly frost-bitten. Harriett, from her own place of concealment, entered into communication with him & brot. him off.

At "Camp Meeting time," the following summer, she again went back, & went, as before, into concealment. She had interviews with the three brothers, but they all refused to leave the man who had been so kind to them, & at his own risk of loss by hiring their time put off the day of sale. To leave him then would have been a loss to him of the wages of their unexpired service. She did not, however, come away empty-handed but brot. off a young man in the neighborhood, who hearing of her proposed to escape with her.

At Christmas she returned again for her brothers. Their term of service with the lumberman had expired. At Christmas they were to have been sold. On Christmas eve. 1854, she & they left for Canada, where they soon after arrived safely.

—Sydney Howard Gay, *Journal*, 1855–56

She crossed creeks on railroad bridges by night, she hid her company in the woods while she herself not being advertised went into the towns in search of information. If met on the road, her face was always to the south.

—Ednah Dow Cheney, "Moses," *Freedman's Record*, March 1865

They hid in potato holes by day, while their pursuers passed within a few feet of them; they were passed along by friends in various disguises; they scattered and separated; some traveling by boat, some by wagons, some by cars, others on foot, to meet at some specified station of the underground railway.

—Sarah Hopkins Bradford, *Scenes in the Life of Harriet Tubman*

ABOVE: J. Schuchman, "Bridge No. 32.03, Maryland & Delaware Railroad over Tuckahoe Creek," 2011. This later bridge may suggest those in Delaware that Harriet Tubman might have crossed at night—treacherous both in its open spaces between the ties and in its exposure to slave-catchers. *Maryland Historical Trust.*

OPPOSITE: A clearing in the woods, where Underground Railroad conductor Harriet Tubman's passengers might hide in wait for a signal from her. *Charlie Ewers.*

"Sweet Potato Bank." These banks or "potatoe-holes" for storing potatoes could hide people below the floor of a cabin or in the fields, as described by Sarah Bradford Hopkins and Seba Smith. *From the* Times & Democrat *(Orangeburg, SC), December 9, 1979.*

Under a part of the floor, was a small excavation in the earth, which his host called his potato-hole, since, being near the fire, it served in winter to keep his potatoes from freezing....It was Johnson's advice, that the colonel should be secreted in this potato-hole. He was afraid, however, that they would search so close as to discover his retreat. Yet the only alternative seemed between the plan proposed and betaking himself again to the woods, exposed to toil and starvation, and the chance of arrest by some of the hundreds who would be scouring the woods that day, eager as bloodhounds for their prey. Something must be done immediately, for he was expecting every hour to hear the cry of his pursuers; and relying on Johnson's ingenuity and skill to send them off on another scent should they come to his camp, he concluded to retreat to the potato-hole....

A board was taken up from the floor, and the gallant colonel descended to his new quarters. They were small to be sure, but under the circumstances very acceptable. The cell was barely deep enough to receive him in a sitting posture, with his neck a little bent, while under him was a little straw, upon which he could stretch his limbs to rest. Johnson replaced all the articles with such care that no one would have supposed they had been moved for months.

—Seba Smith, *Way Down East*, 1854

There [Harriet Tubman] took them to the house of a colored woman, and for one week they lay concealed there in a potatoe hole.

—Sydney Howard Gay, *Journal*, 1855–56

We laid by until starlight, then we made for a road leading to the north. We would follow a road until it bent away from the north; then we would leave it and go by the compass. This caused us to meet many rivers and streams where there were no bridges; some we could wade over, and some we crossed by swimming. After reaching the clearings, we scarcely dared build a fire. Once or twice we took some green corn from the fields, and made a brush fire to roast it. After lighting the fire, we would retire from it, as far almost as we could see it, and then watch whether anybody might come to it. When the fire had gone out, the corn would be about done.

—Benjamin Drew, "James Adams," *A North-Side View of Slavery*, 1856

She found a friend in a white lady, who knew her story and helped her on her way.

—Franklin B. Sanborn, "Harriet Tubman," the (Boston) *Commonwealth*, July 17, 1863

She came to a cabin of colored people, who took them all in, put them to bed, and dried their clothes, ready to proceed next night on their journey. Harriet had run out of money, and gave them some of her underclothing to pay for their kindness....The strange part of the story we found to be, that the master of these two men had put up the previous day, at the railroad station near where she left, an advertisement for them, offering a large reward for their apprehension; but they made a safe exit.

—Thomas Garrett, in Sarah Hopkins Bradford, *Scenes in the Life of Harriet Tubman*, 1869

For many years no woman living in Philadelphia was better known to the colored people of the city generally, than Esther Moore. No woman, white or colored, living in Philadelphia for the same number of years, left her home oftener, especially to seek out and aid the weary travelers escaping from bondage, than did this philanthropist....For it was her delight to see the fugitives individually, take them by the hand and warmly welcome them to freedom. She literally wept with those who wept, while in tones of peculiar love, sincerity, and firmness, she lauded them for their noble daring, and freely expressed her entire sympathy with them, and likewise with all in the prison-house. She condemned Slavery in all its phases, as a "monster to be loathed as the enemy of God and man."

—William Still, "Esther Moore," *The Underground Rail Road*, 1872

A description of one of the agents who helped passengers on the Underground Railroad.

They met at the house of Sam Green, the man who was afterwards sent to prison for ten years for having a copy of "Uncle Tom's Cabin" in his house.

—Sarah Hopkins Bradford, *Harriet, the Moses of Her People*, 1886

Without knowing whom to trust, or how near the pursuers might be, she carefully felt her way, and by her native cunning, or by God given wisdom, she managed to apply to the right people for food, and sometimes for shelter; though often her bed was only the cold ground, and her watchers the stars of night.

—Sarah Hopkins Bradford, *Harriet, the Moses of Her People*, 1886

On one occasion as she was journeying north with a group in a wagon, they stopped at the home of a supposed colored friend. He was not at home upon their arrival, but his wife fed them and put them to bed in the attic of the house. Harriet was awake when the husband arrived home and his wife informed of a presence of the group in the attic, for she heard him remark, "There is a reward offered for the capture of Harriet and I am going to get it." Thereupon he ate his supper and went in search of the police. As soon as his steps died away, however, Harriet aroused her comrades and they quickly vacated the premises and proceeded safely on their way without apprehension.

—E.U.A. Brooks, "In Memory of Harriet Tubman," circa 1950

Self-liberation might mean "hiding in plain sight," as seen in Bensell, Schell and others, "Escape with a Lady, as her Coachman, with Master's Carriages and Horses," in William Still, "Four Arrivals." *From* The Underground Rail Road, *1872.*

One night she came to a town where she expected to find a friend who had before this given her aid. She left her party huddled together in the street in a pouring rain, and advancing to the door of the house where she had formerly visited she gave a peculiar rap, which she knew her friend would recognize. A white man put his head out of the window and gruffly demanded what she wanted. She asked for her acquaintance, and was told that he had been forced to leave there for "harboring niggers."

Daylight was close at hand. Discovery seemed imminent; but Harriet hesitated only a moment before she remembered a swamp lying near the village, and into its recesses she led the slaves. They lay down in the tall, damp grass. They were hungry and they were frightened, but Harriet dared not go for food, lest the man she had roused should have suspected her and set officers on the search. There was a pair of twin babies in the party, but they were drugged, and knew not the danger and discomfort of the situation. The adults knew and they shivered through the long dismal day.

After night fell again, a man dressed in Quaker clothes came walking along the edge of the swamp. He talked in a low tone as if to himself, and sharp ears listened. Harriet heard him say: "My wagon stands in the barn-yard of the next farm across the way. The horse is in the stable; the harness hangs on a nail."

So murmuring, the stranger passed on. Night settled over the world. Harriet stole away to the farmyard. There she found the wagon; and it was stocked with provisions. In a very brief space of time, she was driving her whole party to the next stopping place on the Underground Railroad.

She gave the horse and wagon in charge to a Quaker there, who doubtless found the owner and returned them to him. But Harriet never learned how the stranger knew that the fugitives were lurking in the swamp, nor did she greatly care to know. She always expected God to send her deliverance in time of trouble, and she saw no reason for wondering that He had done so this time.

—Lillie B. Chace Wyman, "Harriet Tubman," *New England Magazine*, March 1896

ABOVE: Anon., "F Stands for *Fugitives* hasting from wrath," in "Iron Gray," illustrating Gray's line "A refuge they seek in the hideous swamp," similarly described by Lillie B. Chace Wyman's account of Harriet Tubman conducting her passengers away from danger when a safe house was no longer a refuge. *From* The Gospel of Slavery, *1864.*

CLARA SMALL

When Harriet Tubman left Dorchester County, she did not expect to see her family again. She knew that leaving could mean reprisals for her relatives. Yet the family was already torn apart. Three sisters had been sold south. The family would not see or hear from them again.

The family structure was fragile in slavery. Harriet Tubman was unusual in that she knew and had contact with both her father and mother. But enslaved families depended on the whim and economic situation of the owner. The whole family could be sold off.

Leaving for the North could make matters worse. Reverend Samuel Green lost track of his daughter Sarah when she was sold south by Dr. James Muse after his son fled with the help of Harriet Tubman. After the Civil War, the Freedmen's Bureau and other agencies would help to reconnect families, working from the surname of the owner. This strategy did not work in the case of Harriet Tubman's sisters or Reverend Samuel Green's daughter.

No doubt this fear of losing family played a role when Harriet Tubman and her brothers Ben and Henry first ran away from Poplar Neck. They returned soon after. They were worried about those reprisals against their family— especially Ben's wife and children.

So when Harriet Tubman decided to leave Dorchester on her own, she was making a drastic decision. Since she was married, her husband, John Tubman, would tell on her to avoid reprisals. He would later even take a new wife. As for Harriet Tubman, she decided to live free or die trying. She was willing to lose everything.

She knew that she might not see her family ever again. But she also realized that her family's situation was fragile, because Edward Brodess had been troubled with debts. The future of Harriet Tubman's family depended on economics.

In leaving for the North, she knew the Dorchester landscape because she had worked it. She knew the water. She knew the topography. If you knew the immediate area, you could find the rest of the way, since it was not that different. In addition, she was assisted by others, including the Quakers, who provided shelter and directions for the travelers.

Others were not so helpful. Some fugitive enslaved persons would return and reveal how they fled. Some people who offered to help you would capture you to sell you south. Patty Cannon and her gang established a reverse Underground Railroad in this way.

You can therefore see why Harriet Tubman was known as "General Tubman" on the Underground Railroad before her days in the Civil War. She was responsible for food, shoes, clothing, shelter. She practiced leadership as if she were an officer in the army. If one of her "passengers" went "AWOL," she would bring him or her back. That is why she never lost a person on her convoys to the North.

You can see why John Brown planned his campaign with General Tubman playing a lead role. She would have helped to rally poor white farmers, as well as enslaved and free African Americans. When she did actually go to war, she played a major role in the Union army's Combahee River Raid, rescuing 756 formerly enslaved people from the plantations along the river and seeing to their protection.

When we talk about Maryland history, we must talk about Harriet Tubman and Frederick Douglass—one from Dorchester County, the other from Talbot County. Their descendants still cherish their memory, and we should do the same. Dorchester County natives such as Bill Jarmon are helping to educate others about Harriet Tubman's legacy and the legacy of slavery by working with her descendants, preserving the history.

After the death of Harriet Tubman, there arose another legacy of racism and discrimination from the 1920s, 1930s and 1940s. The civil rights movement of the 1950s and 1960s left a different and positive legacy of cooperation, leading the way to ensure that a people would not have to go through an experience like that again. We must use the same approach for the next generation, recognizing that education is the way to alleviate our problems. We can do that by understanding each other's history. Harriet Tubman is a key part of that understanding—both here in Dorchester County and everywhere in the United States.

As I look at this landscape, I think about Harriet Tubman risking all by coming back. Her knowledge of this landscape was her power to do this, taking on many forms. While others did not go far, she went the distance and back several times.

That was the strength of her desire for freedom. It meant so much to her. It should be the same for all of us. If we don't pay attention and act, we will lose what has been gained.

—CLARA SMALL, PhD
Professor Emerita, Salisbury University

10

Through the Deep Waters

SHOWING HEEDLESS DARING AND QUICK WIT

On the "Seaboard Line" of the Underground Railroad plied by Harriet Tubman, many routes led to Philadelphia and the North—trails such as this, country roads, railroad beds and bridges, steamboats and trains and—when necessary—river and stream crossings and bushwhacking parallel to those rivers and streams that led to the Northeast and freedom. *Charlie Ewers.*

She operated along the Eastern, or Seaboard, line of the Underground Railroad throughout the 1850's. In those ten years, she plotted innumerable excursions and conducted some twenty major raids to smuggle Negroes out of the Southern States. She was the despair of the slave patrols, who for many years did not even know who she was. Broadsides and dodgers advertising her for capture referred to her as a man, the black-hunters being deceived, perhaps, by her sobriquet of Moses or by some other nickname, General Tubman, admirably bestowed upon her by John Brown in recognition of her strategical ability.

—Samuel Hopkins Adams, *Grandfather Stories*, 1947

⚬

She came to Philadelphia, and worked in hotels, in club houses, and afterwards at Cape May. Whenever she had raised money enough to pay expenses, she would make her way back, hide herself, and in various ways give notice to those who were ready to strike for freedom. When her party was made up, they would start always on Saturday night, because advertisements could not be sent out on Sunday, which gave them one day in advance.

—Sarah Hopkins Bradford, *Scenes in the Life of Harriet Tubman*, 1869

OPPOSITE, TOP LEFT: The Underground Railroad was celebrated in sheet music, as seen in George N. Allen, "Song of the Fugitive," 1854. *The Lester S. Levy Sheet Music Collection, Johns Hopkins University.*

OPPOSITE, TOP RIGHT: "Fr.H.," "Underground Railroad March," lithograph by Knoell & Ochsner, 1855, showing another piece of sheet music celebrating the Underground Railroad. The cover appears to show a train going into a tunnel, becoming a literal underground railroad. *Library of Congress.*

OPPOSITE, BOTTOM: Charles T. Webber, *The Underground Railroad*, painted for the 1893 Columbian Exposition, Cincinnati Art Museum. The painting illustrated a wagonload of fugitives arriving at the home of Levi Coffin, who wrote that "the [railroad was] always in running order, the connections were good, the conductors active and zealous, and there was no lack of passengers....We found it necessary to be always prepared to receive such company and properly care for them." (Levi Coffin, *Reminiscences*, 1876.) *Wikimedia Commons.*

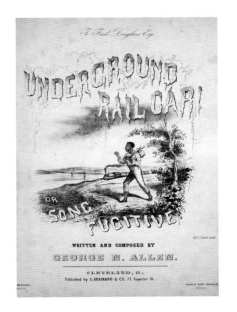

One hundred runaway slaves reach [Boston] every year by means of the "underground railway." Some remain there—others go to Canada. The underground railway is simply an arrangement with individuals along certain routes, to whom the slaves have letters of introduction and by whom they are provided with means and funds to aid them on their way from one place to another.

—From the *Boston Traveller*, quoted in *The St. Johnsbury Caledonian*, February 5, 1848

⚬

His master followed in hot pursuit, to the Ohio river, which divides the slave from the free States; here he lost the track of his escaped chattel, not knowing, or having the least idea as to, the direction the slave had taken; he therefore, gave up all hope of his recovery. Being disappointed, and the loser of a thousand dollars, and having no object on which to vent his dirty spleen, he turned upon the poor Abolitionists, and said—"The d—d Abolitionists must have a railroad under the ground by which they run off niggers."

The significant term "underground" emanated from this circumstance. Of course, up to the present time the slaveholders have not succeeded in locating this useful road, which is therefore as much concealed from them as though it was literally under the ground; consequently it is denominated "underground." And the means by which the slaves still disappear, like the one just alluded to, beyond the probability of recovery, so suddenly, and with such rapid progress, we very appropriately call a railroad. This is the derivation of the term "Underground Railroad."

—William M. Mitchell, *The Underground Railroad from Slavery to Freedom*, 1860

The Underground Railroad. No railroad in the world deserves greater encouragement than the one which bears this name, at once so peculiar and so expressive. It was originally projected to connect the Southern States of the American Union with the Northern: Slavery with Freedom.

The line has been constructed with admirable skill, as they can testify whose circumstances have compelled them to avail themselves of this mode of transit....Once the passenger is fairly on the line, he seldom fails reaching his ultimate destination. Owing to the great danger and the numerous difficulties that attend the running of a train, extreme caution is requisite in regulating the hour of its departure, and no small amount of ingenuity and dexterity is brought into play to secure the safety of the passengers. The mode of conveyance varies according to circumstances and the exigencies of the case; but in this respect, comfort is disregarded as a matter of trifling importance, in comparison with the principal object, which is individual security. The underground railroad being for the exclusive use of slaves, who are running for freedom, its managers are not known, in a general way. It is rather a point with them to evade popularity, for detection would bring with it no end of fines and imprisonment. Yet they derive no pecuniary advantage from what is called "the forwarding business." They work, like noble heroes as they are, for suffering and oppressed humanity, and for no other reward than the satisfaction of their conscience.

—*Anti-Slavery Reporter*, "The Underground Railroad," April 1, 1853

The earnest men of the different stations from time to time received Grape Vine telegraph dispatches and were always ready to act with promptness in facilitating the onward progress of the fugitive.

—Rush R. Sloane, "The Underground Railroad of the Firelands," *The Firelands Pioneer*, May-October 1888

From the time that Garrison, Lovejoy, and others began to agitate for freedom, the slaves throughout the South kept in close touch with the progress of the movement. Though I was a mere child during the preparation for the Civil War and during the war itself, I now recall the many late-at-night whispered discussions that I heard my mother and the other slaves on the plantation indulge in. These discussions showed that they understood the situation, and that they kept themselves informed of events by what was termed the "grape-vine" telegraph.

—Booker T. Washington, *Up from Slavery*, 1900

She assumed the authority and enforced the discipline of a military despot....Under her direction the women were burdened like herself, while she uplifted them with an eloquence born of a noble nature.

—Frank C. Drake, "The Moses of Her People," *New York Herald*, 1907

The expedition was governed by the strictest rules. If any man gave out, he must be shot. "Would you really do that?" she was asked. "Yes," she replied, "if he was weak enough to give out, he'd be weak enough to betray us all, and all who had helped us; and do you think I'd let so many die just for one coward man." "Did you ever have to shoot any one?" [she] was asked. "One time," she said, "a man gave out the second night; his feet were sore and swollen, he couldn't go any further; he'd rather go back and die, if he must." They tried all arguments in vain, bathed his feet, tried to strengthen him, but it was of no use, he would go back. Then she said, "I told the boys to get their guns ready, and shoot him. They'd have done it in a minute; but when he heard that, he jumped right up and went on as well as any body."

—Ednah Dow Cheney, "Moses," *The Freedmen's Record*, March 1865

ABOVE: "Twenty-Eight Fugitives Escaping from the Eastern Shore of Maryland," in William Still , "The Arrivals of a Single Month." *From* The Underground Rail Road, *1872.*

So she compelled them to drag their weary limbs on their northward journey.

—Sarah Hopkins Bradford, *Harriet, the Moses of Her People*, 1886

In one instance, when she had two stout men with her, some 30 miles below here, she said that God told her to stop, which she did; and then asked him what she must do. He told her to leave the road, and turn to the left; she obeyed, and soon came to a small stream of tide water; there was no boat, no bridge; she again inquired of her Guide what she was to do. She was told to go through. It was cold, in the month of March; but having confidence in her Guide, she went in; the water came up to her arm-pits; the men refused to follow till they saw her safe on the opposite shore. They then followed, and if I mistake not, she had soon to wade a second stream.

—Thomas Garrett, letter to Sarah Bradford Hopkins, 1868

"And den how we laughed," said she. "We was the fools and *dey* was de wise men, but we wasn't fools enough to go down de high road in de broad daylight."

—Sarah Hopkins Bradford, *Scenes in the Life of Harriet Tubman*, 1869

She may have avoided the high road, but Harriet Tubman used both steamboats and railroads in broad daylight as a conductor on the Underground Railroad.

Once she sent her company of fugitives onward by some secret route, and started North herself on a railroad train. There were posters in the car offering $40,000 for her head. The passengers read these papers aloud, so that she learned their purport. At the next station, the dauntless woman left the car and took a train going South, feeling convinced that no one would suspect that a woman upon whose life a price was set would dare turn her face in that direction.

—Lillie Chase Wyman, "Harriet Tubman," *New England Magazine*, 1896

Another time she was on the train, and as she says, "Dere I was a settin when I turned and saw ole Massa. But some man had lef' a newspaper in my seat, an I pick it up an hel' it in front of my face—an—I don't know yit whether it was bottom side up or not; but he knew I couldn't read an' so didn't 'spect me, an' de lord save me that time too."

—Emma Paddock Telford, *Harriet: The Modern Moses of Heroism and Visions*, circa 1905

I asked her if she was not frightened.... "Not a bit," she said. She knew she would get off safe.

—Thomas Garrett, letter to Eliza Wigham, 1856

She had gone to Philadelphia with the captain of a steamboat, trading through the Delaware & Chesapeake Canal, and had taken the precaution to get from him a certificate of her being a resident of Philadelphia and free....

[She] took passage for herself and her companion on the Eastern Shore of Maryland, in the steamboat...and knowing the captain of the boat that took her to Baltimore, [she knew that the other captain] was on to give her a certificate, also.

—Thomas Garrett, letter to Eliza Wigham, 1856

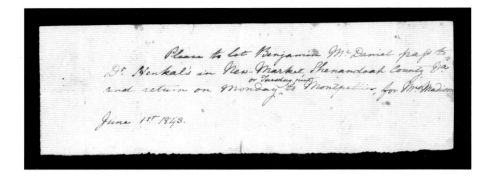

"Don't I tell you, Missus, 'twan't *me*, 'twas *de Lord*! Jes' so long as he wanted to use me, he would take keer of me, an' when he didn't want me no longer, I was ready to go; I always tole him, I'm gwine to hole stiddy on to you, an' you've got to see me trou."

—Sarah Hopkins Bradford, *Harriet, the Moses of Her People*, 1886

ABOVE: Harriet Tubman would obtain passports—documents occasionally issued to free African Americans or trusted enslaved people on the Eastern Shore—to enable her and some of her passengers to travel on steamboat or train. Pictured is a slave pass for Benjamin McDaniel to travel from Montpellier to New Market, Shenandoah County, Virginia, June 1, 1843. *Middleton A. "Spike" Harris Papers, Schomburg Center, New York Public Library.*

NOTICE.

On and after the 1st of October, 1856, the
STEAMER *KENT*, Captain A.B. Fields, will run
her trips as follows:
Monday leave Denton for Baltimore at 7 A.M.
Tuesday leave Baltimore for Seaford at 7 A.M.
Wednesday, leave Seaford for Baltimore at 7 A.M.
Wednesday night leave Baltimore for Denton at 12.
Thursday leave Denton for Baltimore at 12 M.
Friday lay day.
Saturday leave Baltimore for Denton at 7 A.M.
Fare to Denton and landings on the Choptank
River, $2.00
Round trip tickets 3.00
Fare to Seaford and landings on Nanticoke, 2.50
[Fare to] Hooper's Straits, 2.00
Meals extra. All freight pre-paid.
Leaves Baltimore from No. 1 State Tobacco
Warehouse, Dugan's wharf
C.K. CANNON, Clerk.

(Baltimore) *Sun*, November 28, 1856

The boat on which they had expected to leave was disabled, and another boat was to take its place....Among her many friends, there was one who seemed to have influence with the clerk of the boat, on which she expected to take passage; and she was the bearer of a note requesting, or commanding him to take these two women to the end of his route, asking no questions.

Now here was an unforeseen difficulty; the boat was not going; the clerk was not there; all on the other boat were strangers. But forward they must go, trusting in Providence....

They joined the stream of people going up to get their tickets, but when Harriet asked for hers, the clerk eyed her suspiciously, and said: "You just stand aside, you two; I'll attend to your case bye and bye."

Harriet led the young girl to the bow of the boat, where they were alone, and here, having no other help, she, as was her custom, addressed herself to the Lord.

Kneeling on the seat, and supporting her head on her hands, and fixing her eyes on the waters of the bay, she groaned:

"Oh, Lord! You've been wid me in six troubles, *don't* desert me in the seventh!"

"Moses! Moses!" cried Tilly, pulling her by the sleeve. "Do go and see if you can't get tickets now."

"Oh, Lord! You've been wid me in six troubles, *don't* desert me in the seventh."

And so Harriet's story goes on in her peculiarly graphic manner, till at length in terror Tilly exclaimed:

"Oh, Moses! the man is coming. What shall we do?"

"Oh, Lord, you've been wid me in six troubles!"

Here the clerk touched her on the shoulder, and Tilly thought their time had come, but all he said was:

"You can come now and get your tickets," and their troubles were over.

—Sarah Hopkins Bradford, *Harriet, the Moses of Her People*, 1886

But the strangest thing about this woman is, she does not know, or appears not to know, that she has done anything worth notice! May her Guardian continue to preserve her many perilous adventures.

—Thomas Garrett, letter to Eliza Wigham, 1856

The Delaware Railroad, lately opened, is said to be doing an excellent business.

—(Baltimore) *Sun*, March 19, 1856

When the boat arrived in Seaford, she boldly went to the Hotel and called for supper and lodging. Next morning, when they were about to leave, a dealer in such stock attempted to arrest them, but on showing the captain's certificate, the landlord interfered and the woman paid for passage to Camden [Delaware], some 50 miles below here [Wilmington, Delaware], and then came up in private conveyance.

—Thomas Garrett, letter to Eliza Wigham, 1856

ABOVE: "Chesapeake Bay Steamboat *Emma Giles*, 1887" in Samuel Ward Stanton. Launched in 1887, the *Emma Giles* gives us an impression of the steamers operating on Chesapeake Bay in the mid- to late nineteenth century. These boats would have connected Harriet Tubman's Dorchester native land to Baltimore, Maryland, and Seaford, Delaware, via the Choptank and Nanticoke Rivers. *From* American Steam Vessels, *1895*.

"I wouldn't trust Uncle Sam wid my
people no longer; I brought 'em all clar off
to Canada."

—Sarah Hopkins Bradford, *Scenes in the Life of Harriet Tubman*, 1869

ABOVE: "Railroad Town" (Felton Station), 1873. This station, built in 1868, dates from after
the time when Harriet Tubman made use of the Delaware Railroad, which had reached Felton
in 1856. Harriet Tubman was well informed of the progress of the railroad and likely made use
of it before slave catchers routinely would have patrolled it. *Delaware Public Archives*.

OPPOSITE: "The Only Route via Niagara Falls and the Suspension Bridge," circa 1876. The
Niagara Falls Suspension Bridge, built in 1855, would have taken Harriet Tubman and Josiah
"Joe" Bailey to Canada. *Library of Congress*.

"And how far is it now to Canada?" he asked. When told how many miles, for they were to come through New York State, and cross the Suspension Bridge, [Josiah "Joe" Bailey] was ready to give up. "From dat time Joe was silent," said Harriet; "he sang no more, he talked no more; he sat wid his head on his hand, and nobody could 'muse him or make him take any interest in any ting." They passed along in safety, and at length found themselves in the cars, approaching Suspension Bridge. The rest were very joyous and happy, but Joe sat silent and sad.... Harriet and all their party lifted up their voices and sang....

The cars began to cross the bridge. Harriet was very anxious to have her companions see the Falls. William, Peter, and Eliza came eagerly to look at the wonderful sight; but Joe sat still, with his head upon his hand.

"Joe, come look at de Falls! Joe, you fool you, come see de Falls! its your last chance." But Joe sat still and never raised his head. At length Harriet knew by the rise in the center of the bridge, and the descent on the other side that they had crossed "the line." She sprang across to Joe's seat, shook him with all her might, and shouted, "Joe, you've shook de lion's paw!" Joe did not know what she meant. "Joe, you're free!" shouted Harriet. Then Joe's head went up, he raised his hands on high, and his face, streaming with tears, to heaven, and broke out in loud and thrilling tones:

"Glory to God and Jesus too,
One more soul is safe!
Oh, go and carry de news,
One more soul got safe."

"Joe, come and look at de Falls!" called Harriet.

"Glory to God and Jesus too,
One more soul got safe."

was all the answer. The cars stopped on the other side. Joe's feet were the first to touch British soil, after those of the conductor.

"The ladies and gentlemen gathered round him," said Harriet, "till I couldn't see Joe for the crowd, only I heard 'Glory to God and Jesus too!' louder than ever." William went after him, and pulled him, saying, "Joe, stop your noise! You act like a fool!" Then Peter ran in and jerked him mos' off his feet,—"Joe, stop your hollerin'! Folks'll think you're crazy!" But Joe gave no heed. The ladies were crying, and the tears like rain ran down Joe's sable cheeks. A lady reached over her fine cambric handkerchief to him. Joe wiped his face, and then he spoke.

"Oh! if I'd felt like dis down South, it would hab taken nine men to take me; only one more journey for me now, and dat is to Hebben!" "Well, you ole fool you," said Harriet, with whom there seems but one step from the sublime to the ridiculous, "you might a' looked at de Falls fast, and den gone to Hebben afterwards."

—Sarah Hopkins Bradford, *Scenes in the Life of Harriet Tubman*, 1869

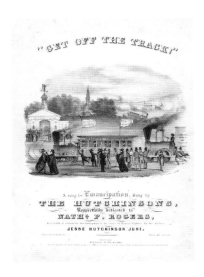

Jesse Hutchinson Jr., "Get off the Track, A Song for Emancipation," 1844, another railroad-related theme. Looking beyond the allegory of the image, one might imagine Josiah "Joe" Bailey arriving in Canada with Harriet Tubman. *Library of Congress*.

I heard old Queen Victoria say,
If we would all forsake
Our native land and slavery,
And come across the lake,
That she was standing on the shore,
With arms extended wide,
To give us all a peaceful home
Beyond the rolling tide.
O, old master, don't come after me,
For I'm on my way to Canada,
Where colored men are free

—"Away to Canada" (verse), Joshua McCarter Simpson, *Original Anti-slavery Songs*, 1852

This was the song sung by Harriet Tubman and her companions when crossing the Niagara Falls Suspension Bridge.

With an almost heedless daring, she went to the very village
where lived one of her old masters, to whom she had been hired.
Stopping at the market long enough to buy a pair of live fowls
she tied them together by the legs, and pulling her sunbonnet
well over her face started down the village street. Just before
reaching a corner and too late to beat a retreat, she spied her
old master coming toward her. "Quick as a flash" to use her
own words, and Harriet always laughs most heartily as she
recounts this adventure "I loosened de string dat held dair laigs,
an pinch dem pore chickens tel day squawk an' flutter like deys
gwine to git away from me an I had all I could do to hole on
to um; an' as I wuz busy a bendin my haid down' an' keepin'
un goin' I could see ole massa laugh to see what a time dem
chickens was makin', an he neber spicioned dat it was Mrs.
Harriet he wanted so bad dat was right dere under his eyes."

—Emma Paddock Telford, *Harriet: The Modern Moses of Heroism and Visions*,
circa 1905

ABOVE: Kilburn Brothers, "The Merry Market Maid, Washington, D.C., U.S.A.," circa 1889.
Harriet Tubman would have been skilled in blending in with a crowd in a town, even if she
could have been recognized there. *Library of Congress*.

Several times she was at the point of being taken but always escaped by her quick wit.

—Emma Paddock Telford, *Harriet: The Modern Moses of Heroism and Visions*, circa 1905

At another time she was being questioned too closely on a stage coach, by men who were looking for her and she said: "Gentlemen, let me sing for you"—she had a great voice for song—then sang on for mile after mile 'till they came to the next station, then bade them good-bye, and left the stage.

—*Auburn Citizen*, "Two Timely Topics," 1913

Once she and a band of eleven when crossing a bridge came upon a company of Irish laborers: What to do? Being asked what was her business, she said her present speculation was getting a husband. She had had one colored husband and she meant to marry a white gentleman next time. This made a great laugh so they went on thro' the town together laughing and talking.

—Emily Howland, *Diary*, 1873

At another time when she heard men talking about her, she pretended to read a book which she carried. One man remarked, "This can't be the woman. The one we want can't read or write." Harriet devoutly hoped this book was right side up.

—Helen Woodruff Tatlock, interview, 1939

WILMINGTON, DEL.
1874.

It was a wise plan of our sagacious heroine to leave her old parents till the last to be brought away. They were pensioned off as too old to work, had a cabin, and a horse and cow, and were quite comfortable....But at length Harriet heard that the old man had been betrayed by a slave whom he had assisted, but who had turned back, and when questioned by his wife, told her the story of his intended escape, and of the aid he had received from "Old Ben." This woman, hoping to curry favor with her master, revealed the whole to him, and "Old Ben" was arrested. He was to be tried the next week, when Harriet appeared upon the scene, and, as she says, "saved dem de expense ob de trial," and removed her father to a higher court, by taking him off to Canada.

—Sarah Hopkins Bradford, *Scenes in the Life of Harriet Tubman*, 1869

ABOVE: "Wilmington, Delaware," 1874, where Harriet Tubman "made a great laugh" with the Irish laborers crossing the bridge on the Christina River on the way to Pennsylvania. *Wikipedia Commons.*

OPPOSITE: A later nineteenth-century African American wagon driver, "Stagecoach" Mary Fields. *Ursuline Sisters Archives.*

When she found her mother unwilling to leave behind her feather-bedtick, and her father his broad-axe and other tools, she bundled up bed-tick, broad-axe, mother, father, all, and landed them in Canada.

—Robert W. Taylor, "Harriet Tubman–The Heroine in Ebony," 1901

She brought away her aged parents in a singular manner. They started with an old horse, fitted out in primitive style with a straw collar, a pair of old chaise wheels, with a board on the axle to sit on, another board swung with ropes, fastened to the axle, to rest their feet on. She got her parents, who were both slaves belonging to different masters, on this rude vehicle to the railroad, put them in the cars, turned Jehu herself, and drove to town in a style that no human being ever did before or since; but she was happy at having arrived safe....I believe that Harriet succeeded in freeing all her relatives but one sister and her three children.

—Thomas Garrett, in Sarah Hopkins Bradford, *Scenes in the Life of Harriet Tubman*, 1869

LINDA DUYER

When I think about Harriet Tubman conducting on the Underground Railroad in Dorchester County, I visualize her crossing narrow streams, doing a lot of wading. She would know the best places to cross and when the water would be low. She would do this when she needed to avoid the roads and rivers that were the highways of the time where she would be seen easily. Her view of the landscape was shaped by water, influencing where she could go and where she could hide.

She "toted a map in her head" of Dorchester and the Mid-Shore because she went all over the area with her father in the timber business. She knew where the timber would be carried by water, by river or canal. She knew Cambridge, Madison and Preston. She did a lot of walking in her work. She lived in several places along the way.

She also knew how to get about secretly. She could move without notice between properties to worship and socialize. She may have known crossings from Black watermen who made a living from the rivers and creeks. She would have known the trails—some of them going back to the Indians—that went down and across the "necks" of high ground. These were well-worn paths for people white and Black to move between settlements. Since she generally didn't work in the household, she took these trails in her work by day. She also knew the landowners who might be on the lookout. And she knew where she would not be detected. By day or by night, getting from Point A to Point B would not necessarily be on a straight line but shaped by the land and the people on that land.

She knew that freedom was to the north. She would have known of people who left what was known as "Egypt" and never came back. Her mental map may have had a limited description of Delmarva beyond her direct experience. Yet she knew how people must have departed for the north. She knew how their paths were shaped by water on several sides. The rivers pointed northeast. She knew that escape would have carried her in that direction into Delaware on her way north to the headwaters of the Choptank and Nanticoke Rivers.

Charlie Ewers.

In addition, she was better connected than most through her work with her father. She knew the local African American families, as well as the families of the property owners she worked for. Her experience with these families helped her to get the big picture.

When she was leaving "Egypt" and later conducting on the Underground Railroad, she knew who to approach who would be like-minded and supportive. She would know the families willing to hide her and her "passengers," and she would know those who she should avoid. In turn those families would share their knowledge of the wider network with her so she could find people she could trust up the line.

As we know from reading her stories, this knowledge did not eliminate the risk of what she did. She had committed herself to danger and to being killed. In many ways, she was already "dead" to her family, who had never expected to see her again when she departed on her many trips as conductor on the Railroad.

This courage in the face of risk made her bold and brave enough to use whatever means necessary to get from point to point. She took passage on steamboats and trains when necessary. She earned the money to do this between trips in the north. She carried the forged papers to make it through any investigation. Finally, she would rely on her instincts to be safe—even changing trains and traveling deeper into "Egypt" when she thought she was being pursued.

In this way, she could take advantage of the fact that free and enslaved African Americans often had freedom of movement north. She could travel in public as other African Americans did.

Finally, she had that talent for blending into the scenery and escaping notice. She went about in towns and cities without drawing attention to herself. She even walked the streets of Cambridge, Maryland, in her native land and met up with the man who knew her well—distracting him by releasing a chicken under her arm just as she passed him.

How could an ordinary person bring herself to do what she did and then continue doing it again and again? She was not the only person to flee "Egypt," but she had to be knowledgeable and dogged to be successful several times. Anyone who did this over and over again must have been fearless and special. She might have taught others, but she carried people out herself.

Her talents—once hidden to the world—were later revealed for all to learn about: her ability to read people, to disguise herself, to be thinking one step ahead of the situation about what would work. These talents came from someone who had been watchful all her life. Someone who had soaked up knowledge and situations. And she "toted" this all in her head: the environment, the geography and the people. It was this mental map that ensured that her mission would not be a failure.

—LINDA DUYER,
Late Assistant Director, Julia D. Purnell Museum, Snow Hill, Maryland
Independent history researcher, freelance writer and author

11

Tribute Is Finally Being Paid

DORCHESTER REDISCOVERS HARRIET TUBMAN AND HER LEGACY

Charlie Ewers.

Old timers living in Bucktown today do not recall ever hearing of Harriet Tubman. Indeed, the very place where she made history did not even mark or pay tribute to this woman of courage.

—Brice Stump, "Marker Erected in Honor of World Famous Slave," *Dorchester News*, May 3, 1967

FRIEND OF LINCOLN'S DYING

Aged Pilot of Escaping Slaves Suffering from Pneumonia

Auburn, N.Y., March 11.—Harriet Tubman, a colored woman, ninety-five years old, who is said to have been a friend of Abraham Lincoln and Secretary of State William H. Seward, and who was associated with John Brown in anti-slavery work, is dying here of pneumonia.

Harriet Tubman is said to have been connected with the "underground railroad" system by which fleeing slaves were aided in eluding pursuit by slave dealers. It is said that she herself piloted over 300 slaves into Canada by this method.

Reporting a friendship with Abraham Lincoln that falsely embellished the account, this article from the (Dorchester) *Daily Banner* of March 11, 1913, came from an Associated Press Night Wire that was printed virtually unchanged by dozens of newspapers, including the *Banner*. With the exception of descendants of the Green, Ross and Tubman families, Harriet Tubman had been virtually forgotten by the people of Dorchester.

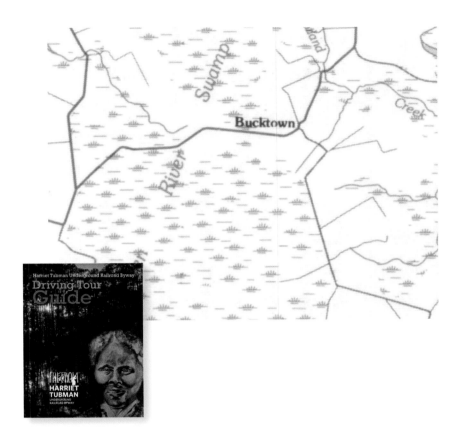

TOP: U.S. Soil Conservation Service, Dorchester County, Maryland, 1979. The Brodess Farm Site (pictured on page 263) is identified by signs from the Maryland Civil War Centennial Commission and the National Underground Railroad Network to Freedom as the home of Edward and Eliza Brodess, who claimed ownership of Harriet Tubman. The connection of the site with the enslaved Ross family, along with much of the memory of Harriet Tubman, was largely forgotten by the time of Harriet Tubman's death in 1913. Charles, Benjamin B. and Thomas J. Brodess acquired the farm from their sisters and brother after the death of their widowed mother, Eliza. The three brothers maintained the farm until 1907, when it passed in succession to two families while it was rented by Milton M. Malkus, whose sons bought the property in 1953. The Brodess farmhouse, which was said to have been located behind the present buildings, has not survived. A part of Blackwater Farms Inc., the property is still farmed by the Malkus family and rented out seasonally to hunters. The signs were added in 1967 and 2013. *Library of Congress, Geography and Map Division.*

INSET: *Harriet Tubman Underground Railroad Byway Driving Map, Site 16.*

I was almost out of school when they was talkin' about Harriet Tubman then. I was born in 1911, and Harriet, she died in 1913 and up in New York.

And then, later on in years, when I was eighty-six, people said I was the oldest Ross livin' that was a relation to her. They told about she bein' in slavery and that she led her family north to Philadelphia....

A lot of people didn't know her real name. They only knew her as Moses. I was raised in the neighborhood where she was busy, at Blackwater. There were a lot of stories, but I forgot 'em.

—Nicey Ross Ennals, in Hal Roth, *Two Pieces of Clothes*, 2003

The Orchid Garden:...Earl Conrad's book *Harriet Tubman*. It's about history's "greatest Negress...."

—Walter Winchell, "On Broadway," September 15, 1944

Modern dictionaries consider "offensive" the use of Winchell's racist, gender-specific "N-word" to describe Harriet Tubman—also seen below.

Who is Harriet Tubman? That's a question that any reader might well be expected to ask, and it would be no show of ignorance not to know the answer. Still, she was an important figure in the freeing of slaves....That's the woman whose biography Earl Conrad writes in *Harriet Tubman*.

Such a dominant personality can't help but having color, and the author presents her story with extreme care to facts and figures. The research must have required extreme patience and the result is a book which will probably not give the monetary reward the task justifies.

—D.M.F., "A Great Negress," *Hartford Courant*, September 12, 1943

An outstanding book has been written by Earl Conrad of this state of the great colored personage.

—(Dorchester) *Daily Banner*, "Charles Cornish Representative at Ship Launching," June 7, 1944

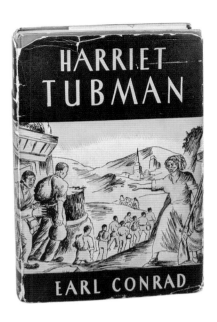

LEFT: Cover of Earl Conrad, *Harriet Tubman*, 1943. Earl Conrad's articles and books about Harriet Tubman revived interest in her life during the early 1940s and helped inspire the naming of a U.S. Liberty ship and a Cambridge ambulance service for African Americans. *Biblio.com.au.*

BELOW: Named for a recently deceased labor leader, the SS *John W. Brown*, one of two Liberty ships still afloat, is berthed in Baltimore Harbor and shown here on a visit to Cambridge, Maryland. It resembles its sister ship, the SS *Harriet Tubman*, launched in 1944. The *Tubman* was the only Liberty ship named for an African American woman—a fitting tribute to Harriet Tubman's military service on the Combahee River during the Civil War. It was built through contributions by the National Council of Negro Women (NCNW) under the leadership of Mary McLeod Bethune, founder and first president. *Charlie Ewers.*

It has come at last, the proper recognition of women in this 20th century of progress. A liberty ship will take to the blue seas...and etched across its steel gray sides will be the name "Harriet Tubman"...the name of a woman whose activities during the Civil War made the background for slave history and the history of free men.

Through the efforts of Mary McLeod Bethune, the Federal Government has seen fit to honor an illustrious Negro woman....We salute you S.S. *Harriet Tubman*.

—*Pittsburgh Courier*, "Liberty Ship S.S. Harriet Tubman," May 20, 1944

ABOVE: While flower girl Miss Hilda Proctor, Harriet Tubman's great-grandniece, looks on, sponsor Mrs. E. Stewart Northrup, grandniece, christens the SS *Harriet Tubman* on June 3, 1944. Office of War Information, "The Launching Party for the S.S. Harriet Tubman," *National Archives*.

Surpassing its $2,000,000 goal by $1,452,000, the National Council of Negro Women announced last week that the SS *Harriet Tubman* has been liberated....A total of $3,452,361.75 bond purchases were credited to the drive.

—*Pittsburgh Courier*, "National Council Surpasses SS Tubman Bond Drive Goal," September 16, 1944

Perhaps most of us have had dreams of grandeur... of wondrous things we yearn to have happen...if not to ourselves, at least to someone we know or wished to have known. One of these dreams tucked far away in the back of our women's minds has been the desire for recognition for some one of us, so that we could say proudly, "Look what we have done."

So this dream came true for us Saturday morning in Portland, Maine, when the Liberty Ship S.S. *Harriet Tubman* made a graceful dip into the ocean and carried the illustrious name into the service of our country.

—Toki Schalk, "A Dream Come True," *Pittsburgh Courier*, June 10, 1944

[Earl Conrad] is partially responsible for the fact the ship will bear the name of this Negro woman, because he brought her to general public attention some months ago with a biography. Harriet Tubman was not widely known except to students of Negro history in America until Conrad's book came out.

—*Aframerican Woman's Journal*, Summer 1944

I am happy to learn that the United States Maritime Commission has named a Liberty Ship in honor of Mrs. Harriet Tubman. This is a fitting honor to a distinguished woman. This Liberty Ship will carry war materials to our fighting men in all parts of the world, where they will be used in defense of those principles that Mrs. Tubman established and which American women now regardless of race, color, or creed are determined to see through to victory. I wish for the National Council of Negro Women and the members of Mrs. Tubman's family success in this important undertaking.

—Eleanor Roosevelt, May 17, 1944, in "Announcement for the Launching of the SS Harriet Tubman"

On Saturday morning *[June 3, 1944]* at South Portland, Maine, a ship was launched by the New England Shipbuilding Corporation in commemoration of Harriet Tubman, a native of Dorchester County, Maryland, having been born at Madison, a woman whose work has gone down in history as a guiding light of Dorchester County as Moses in the freedom that the world is striving to reestablish today.

—(Dorchester) *Daily Banner*, "Charles Cornish Representative at Ship Launching," June 7, 1944

Our county feels greatly honored in having the Maritime Commission, the War Shipping Administration, and the New England Shipbuilding Corporation given consideration in naming a ship in her memory, and also in the recognition of our government in the works of a woman who was born and raised in Dorchester County, and it is with great satisfaction that Mr. Charles Cornish has been selected to represent the County at the launching of a ship bearing the name of Harriet Tubman.

—unidentified Dorchester County commissioner, (Dorchester) *Daily Banner*, "Charles Cornish Representative at Ship Launching," June 7, 1944

ABOVE: Charles E. Cornish, owner of Cornish Transportation and the Charles Cornish Garage, served as president of the Maryland Congress of National Parent Teacher Associations at the time he represented Dorchester County at the launch of the SS *Harriet Tubman*. Two years later, he would be elected to the Cambridge City Council and later be its president. During his life, he would work to desegregate public schools and negotiate for equal opportunity in local businesses. *From Dorchester Tercentenary, 1969.*

In the 1940s, African Americans were not transported by the local ambulance. An old hearse became the Harriet Tubman Ambulance Service. My great-grandfather William Banks helped to organize this when one of his sons was injured and needed to get to the hospital.

—Dion Banks, interview

The Harriet Tubman Ambulance, named in honor of the Underground Railroad hero, was the only one designated to transport African-Americans to the local hospital. People in the community pooled their money together and purchased this carrier in the 1940s.

—"The Harriet Tubman Ambulance," in Pine Street Walking Tour

ABOVE: The Harriet Tubman Ambulance, named in honor of the Underground Railroad hero, was purchased and operated by members of the Cambridge African American community in the 1940s, when they were not served by local ambulance companies. *Courtesy of the family of Evelyn Jones-Banks, from her album.*

OPPOSITE: Mace's Lane School, where the Harriet Tubman Day banquet and program was held on November 2, 1961. *Charlie Ewers.*

All of us should not pay respect or honor Harriet Tubman because she was an ex-slave, a Negro, or because she was a woman but because she was an American, and she stood for, no, fought for, in her own way the high ideals of our American heritage. Harriet Tubman and her work belong not only to the rich heritage of Dorchester, but to the nation and the world.

—William Wroten, "Harriet Tubman Day Address," November 2, 1961

The first secretary and consul to the United States from Liberia spoke last night at the banquet honoring Harriet Tubman to a group of second ward leaders and Cambridge citizens on leadership.

R. Burlington King paid a tribute to the leadership of Harriet Tubman, a slave born in Dorchester County, who from 1849 to the Civil War led over 300 men and women to freedom by means of the Underground Railroad....

The ceremonies concluded a day-long program in Mace's Lane High School here by students and faculty, under the guidance of Miss Edith M. Jolley, principal.

—(Salisbury) *Daily Times*, "Consul from Liberia Honors Harriet Tubman," November 3, 1961

Miss Jolley said last night the purpose of the special day was to draw attention to a Dorchester County woman who had an important part in the course of the national events in the nineteenth century.

—*Dorchester Daily Banner*, "Liberian Diplomat Calls Quality of World Leadership Most Critical," November 3, 1961

She sowed the seeds of freedom
In the hearts of 300 slaves
Helped them to escape the bondage
Of their brutal master knaves
Like Moses, led to Canaan
From the chains and early graves.
Harriet Tubman marches on.

—From "The Harriet Tubman Song" sung at the annual banquets in Cambridge

⚘

Led by Cambridge Nonviolent Action Committee founder Gloria Richardson, the Cambridge Movement sought civil rights and economic opportunities following years of disenfranchisement.

—"Pine Street Walking Tour," Eastern Shore Network for Change

During the turbulent 1960s, Pine Street thrust Cambridge before a worldwide audience when it emerged as one of the most important battlegrounds in the civil rights movement. Gloria Richardson, the daughter of a Cambridge pharmacist, was but one of the home-grown leaders who helped define the movement's goals, first for integration of public accommodations and later for equal treatment in housing, employment, education, and health care.

After protests turned violent in June 1963, the National Guard came in—and imposed martial law for more than a year.

—"Pine Street Walking Tour," Eastern Shore Network for Change

OPPOSITE: "Mrs. Gloria Richardson, head of the Cambridge Nonviolent Action Committee, pushes a National Guardsman's bayonet aside in Cambridge, Maryland on July 21, 1963, as she moves among a crowd of African Americans to convince them to disperse. The crowd gathered after several African Americans attempted to enter a street sealed off by troops. Mrs. Richardson and Fred Jackson, *left*, a CNAC official, made their appeal to the crowd after a tear gas grenade was thrown by the Guard." *AP Photo*.

"City police drag a demonstrator to a patrol car after he and three other persons were arrested during a sit-in demonstration, July 11, 1963, in Cambridge, Maryland. The demonstrator, Dwight Campbell [Cromwell?], 18, of Cambridge, was charged with trespassing, when he refused to leave a segregated lunchroom. The charges later were dropped by the owner." *AP Photo/William A. Smith.*

OPPOSITE, TOP: "Church services have often provided the initial impulse to initiate demands for racial justice and integration. Often civil rights leaders are black clergymen, who inspire the sit-in demonstrations, or kneel-ins. A group of demonstrators kneel outside Cambridge, Maryland, jail, July 19, 1963, to protest imprisonment of fellow demonstrators." *AP Photo.*

OPPOSITE, BOTTOM: The Dorchester District Court today, over fifty years after African Americans once again sought their human rights, echoing Harriet Tubman's words in exile in St. Catharines, Canada, "We would rather stay in our native land if we could be as free there." (Benjamin Drew, *A North-Side View of Slavery,* 1856.) *Charlie Ewers.*

Please sleep in the courthouse and the jail, city hall, and the regular places. Let them know you are not afraid and we shall overcome sooner than you think.

They think they have you scared because they are sending us away, but we aren't afraid. We expect to be out in three months so please fight for freedom and let us know that we are not going away in vain.

—Dinez White, "Letter from a Jail Cell," June 11, 1963

Following the May 1963 "Penny Trials" in which forty-seven civil rights demonstrators were convicted of disorderly conduct and fined one cent, Dinez White and Dwight Cromwell later prayed outside a segregated bowling alley and were arrested for disorderly conduct and sentenced to an indefinite term to state institutions for juveniles.

[Father James Groppi] *said he is often asked what he teaches his young followers, mostly members of the Milwaukee NAACP Youth Council.*

"I teach them black history," he said. "I teach them what Harriet Tubman taught the slaves she helped free many years ago."

And when they would say to her, "Why don't you let me stay? At least I was secure here," [Harriet Tubman] would point a shotgun at them and say, "I'll see you dead before I'll see you a slave."

—Father James Groppi, in Jim Shoop, "Christ Called Civil Rights Worker," *Minneapolis Star*, October 25, 1967

The quote is not a historical one but provides one instance of how Harriet Tubman served as an icon of the civil rights movement in the 1960s.

On the night of July 24, 1967, the Student Nonviolent Coordinating Committee chairman H. Rap Brown appeared in Cambridge at the invitation of local black leaders. He climbed atop a car that night and exhorted Blacks to be more aggressive in their struggle for equality. Several hours later, a fire broke out at Pine Street Elementary School, but firefighters were kept away from the blaze by city officials who feared for their safety after Brown's speech. The fire spread across two square blocks, reducing much of Pine Street's famous downtown to ashes. The cause of the fire has never been firmly established. This single event, however, in many ways came to define Cambridge and its Pine Street community in the national media.

—"Pine Street Walking Tour," Eastern Shore Network for Change

ABOVE: "Armed members of the Maryland National Guard stand watch in the fire-leveled riot area of Cambridge, Md., July 25, 1967, where racial violence erupted during the night. A block-long area was leveled by the flames." *AP Photo/Bob Schutz*.

"She has been called a second Harriet Tubman," *[Dwight]* Cromwell said in his introduction of *[Gloria Richardson]* Dandridge, but Dandridge spoke not about leaders like Tubman, but the need for group leadership....

Dandridge spoke of the recent funeral of civil rights activist Ella Baker....She recalled Baker's words, "Strong people do not need strong leaders."

—Gail Dean, "March Recalls Days Gone By," (Easton) *Star-Democrat*, January 12, 1987

⁊

"Let us today acknowledge the sacrifice and courage left to us by ex-slaves and fellow Dorchester Countians....Let us march in honor of all those people and families who were part of the now-historic Cambridge movement."

—Gloria Richardson Dandridge, quoted in Deborah Barfield, "Dandridge: Success Found in Work of Many, Not One," (Easton) *Star-Democrat*, January 12, 1987

KISHA PETTICOLAS
AND DION BANKS

Charlie Ewers.

Dɪᴏɴ Bᴀɴᴋs: The Dorchester County Courthouse is significant to African American history. The wharf was down High Street from here; the banks and businesses were up the same street. The auctions for enslaved people were here. In 1850, Harriet Tubman's niece Kessiah Jolly Bowley and her two children escaped from the auction block and made their way to Baltimore in a log canoe piloted by her husband, John, where Harriet met them and took them to Philadelphia. H. Rap Brown was indicted here 117 years later in August 1967 for inciting riot and arson in Cambridge the previous month. Later, a bomb went off on the west corner of the building in August 1970, when Brown was to go to trial in Harford County for the 1967 charges.

Kɪsʜᴀ Pᴇᴛᴛɪᴄᴏʟᴀs: In 1857, the court here sentenced Reverend Sam Green to ten years' imprisonment for having in his possession "the incendiary book *Uncle Tom's Cabin*." His son Sam had escaped to Canada with the help of Harriet Tubman a few years before. We suppose this building to be a place of justice. It should be a level playing field. It has not been in the past.

We started the Eastern Shore Network for Change to make safe spaces for these conversations. We want to get these past issues out front and shed light on them. Where we create justice, we can create change.

DB: The center of our work is to tell the African American story here. Harriet Tubman and the Underground Railroad. Gloria Richardson Dandridge of the Cambridge Nonviolent Action Committee, who was arrested and tried here for demonstrations outside segregated

establishments. Dinez White and Dwight Cromwell were also tried here for demonstrations in the same year and sent away to reform schools because of their age. William "Peewee" Jackson was jailed here, too, in 1963 for carrying a knife, until a group of protesters called for his release.

KP: Many people in Cambridge have given us a gut check for celebrating this history. "Why celebrate a thief who stole property?" "Why should a thief have a museum?" This element in the community has grown smaller, but it remains.

DB: How am I inspired by Harriet Tubman? She opened up new horizons with the Underground Railroad. She developed a spirituality connected with the environment. She had a purpose in her work. She knew her destiny.

KP: What is it like living here on the Mid-Shore? Frederick Douglass, Harriet Tubman, Gloria Richardson Dandridge all share this area. And there is still work to be done. Slavery is in the soil. It cannot be undone in a single lifetime. We have had to work in segments: Harriet in her time, Gloria in her time and all of us in our time.

When I am challenged, I think about Harriet and Gloria. They are at the forefront of my mind. I steal from their playbook in dealing with issues. I learn from them that we cannot do everything at once. But we can do what we can do. We can persevere and continue—inspired by a four-foot woman, who garnered an inner strength in her life.

—DION BANKS AND KISHA PETTICOLAS,
Cofounders, Eastern Shore Network for Change

12

"I'm Here, and I'm Going to Stay"

DORCHESTER WELCOMES HOME AND
CELEBRATES HARRIET TUBMAN

Often mistakenly thought of as Harriet Tubman's birthplace, the Brodess Farm Site certainly stands as the most accessible site of Tubman's Dorchester life. Located between her birthplace on Peter's Neck and her first setting-off point in self-liberation at Poplar Neck, it is the centerpiece of Harriet Tubman's "return" to Dorchester County in the mid-twentieth to the early twenty-first centuries after being nearly forgotten after her death. *Charlie Ewers.*

Few people in the Bucktown area are aware of the fact that one of the most famous slaves in the United States lived in their hamlet....It was here that history was made.

—Brice Stump, "Marker Erected in Honor of World Famous Slave," *Dorchester News*, May 3, 1963

ॐ

I was in school at the time of Negro History Week in the first week of February. There would be a banquet at Waugh Chapel. Before that the Harriet Tubman song went back to the 1940s. Edythe Jolley raised money for the Harriet Tubman Ambulance. We couldn't do a whole lot, but we did something. Only one person went to Maine for the launch of the USS Harriet Tubman. That was Charles Cornish.

—Shirley Jackson, trustee, Harriet Tubman Organization

Old timers living in Bucktown today do not recall ever hearing of Harriet Tubman. Indeed, the very place where she made history did not even mark or pay triubute to this woman of Courage.

The farm...is known as the Brodas [sic] Farm. Old timers recall that a large wooden structure stood behind the present house of Mr. & Mrs. William Malkus in the early 1900s. Two brothers by the name of Brodas lived there.

—Brice Stump, "Marker Erected in Honor of World Famous Slave," *Dorchester News*, May 3, 1963

OPPOSITE: Behind the current buildings on the Brodess Farm Site stood the house once occupied by the Brodess family, whose farm was the backdrop for much of Harriet Tubman's life as an enslaved person. Harriet Tubman may have been forgotten by many in Bucktown during the middle of the twentieth century, but she was celebrated not far away at Bazel's Methodist Episcopal Church. *Charlie Ewers.*

The marker may provoke the telling of the legends about this remarkable woman. Well deserved tribute is finally being paid.

—Brice Stump, "Marker Erected in Honor of World Famous Slave," *Dorchester News*, May 3, 1963

Mrs. Mary Pinkett of Cambridge recalled that a picture of Harriet Tubman once hung in the Negro church [Bazel Methodist Episcopal Church] at Bucktown....In the church, Col. Nichols [of the Dorchester Historical Society] found that the top [of the pulpit] could be raised, exposing a small storage area. Intermixed with the various papers was a picture of Harriet Tubman. Once again a legend proved true.

—Brice Stump, "Marker Erected in Honor of World Famous Slave," *Dorchester News*, May 3, 1963

OPPOSITE, TOP: "A historical marker in honor of Dorchester's world famous slave Harriet Tubman has been set up on Greenbriar Rd. at the site of the former Brodas [*sic*] plantation." From Brice Stump, "Marker Erected in Honor of World Famous Slave," *Dorchester News*, May 3, 1963. *Edward H. Nabb Research Center*.

OPPOSITE, BOTTOM: *Left to right*: Brice Stump, "who was instrumental in tracking down the location of the Brodas [*sic*] plantation"; Harriet Tubman descendants Mrs. Elaine Ferrare, Mrs. Mildred C. Griffin, Mrs. Nettie Jolley, Miss Addie Clash and Owens Jackson; and Colonel Walter V. Nichols of the Dorchester Historical Society. From Brice Stump, "Marker Erected in Honor of World Famous Slave," *Dorchester News*, May 3, 1963. *Edward H. Nabb Research Center*.

In the early days before the founding of the organization that would become the Harriet Tubman Organization, local historian Addie Clash Travers was the lady to contact about Harriet Tubman. Locals were given directions to "Ms." Addie's home to those seeking information about the legacy of Harriet Tubman in Dorchester County. Her interest in Harriet Tubman was well received by family members.

Addie Clash Travers persuaded others to celebrate the Harriet Tubman legacy at Bazzel [sic] Church in Bucktown. She was joined by members of the Rev. Richard D. Jackson family in her endeavor. The event was called Harriet Ross Tubman Day, which became an annual activity.

—"About Us," Harriet Tubman Organization website, http://htorganization. blogspot.com/p/blog-page.html

ௐ

Addie Clash Travers founded Harriet Tubman Day, when race riots ripped through Cambridge, county seat of Dorchester County on Maryland's Eastern Shore.

"Sometimes you could count the heads [at annual church services in Tubman's honor]," said Travers, who persevered until, last year, she saw standing room only at the Tubman Ceremonies....

The only official ceremonies honoring Tubman are held each June in the frame churches—one of which was handed down to [former] slaves after their [former] masters built a new church.

—Rebecca Kolbert, "A Determined Few Keep Alive the Legacy of Harriet Tubman," UPI, 1984

This poster, likely associated with the 1940s celebrations of the launching of the SS *Harriet Tubman*, was probably the picture found in Bazel's Methodist Episcopal Church, which helped spur the placement of a marker by the Dorchester County Historical Society nearby at the Brodess Farm Site. *Edward H. Nabb Research Center.*

TOP: "Harriet Tubman's image was there on the tercentenary plate that celebrated Dorchester History." Victoria Jackson-Stanley, former mayor of Cambridge. *Charlie Ewers.*

BOTTOM: This image, likely associated with the Bazel's Church commemorations, was featured on the Dorchester Tercentenary plate. *Charlie Ewers.*

Most people feel festival activities have helped ease racial tensions. Both white and Negro leaders are participating in the celebration.

—Harry Lee, "Cambridge Tercentenary May Help Unity," *Washington Post*, July 17, 1969

Probably nowhere in the United States is there a location where the plight of the Negro has been more profoundly illustrated than here in Dorchester. Ariminta [*sic*] Green—a slave who later became Harriet Tubman, works for the freedom of her people.

—*The Dorchester Story*, Pageant for the Dorchester Tercentenary, July 22–26, 1969

Maryland's Dorchester County and its county seat of Cambridge are plagued with economic problems and a hangover of racial tensions that in 1963 and 1967 exploded in violence.

But this month black and white citizens of the Eastern Shore County are ignoring their past and present troubles and joining in a nostalgic festival in celebration of Dorchester's 300th birthday.

—Harry Lee, "Cambridge Tercentenary May Help Unity," *Washington Post*, July 17, 1969

My parents bought the [tercentenary] plate and hung it on the wall where it stands today. As a young adult, I was impressed and proud to recognize her on the plate. I wanted to be like her.

—Victoria Jackson-Stanley, former mayor of Cambridge, interview

When she came to Dorchester County, Evelyn Townsend from South Carolina asked, "Why don't you have the same feeling about Harriet Tubman?" Harriet Tubman was born to do what she did. I appreciate this organization. It ensures that the legacy left for us should continue. Harriet Tubman loved people and wanted to help others. That's why we're here.

—Ruth Braxton, trustee, Harriet Tubman Organization

The Harriet Tubman Organization began as the Harriet Tubman Association of Dorchester County, which was founded September 24, 1972...to support the early work of co-founders Addie Clash Travers and Rev. Edward Jackson, as the Harriet Tubman Committee....

In 1996, the Board of Directors voted to change its name to the Harriet Tubman Organization, Inc. This change more accurately reflects the group's vision for the future and its revised mission. The mission of the Harriet Tubman Organization is to develop programs and services for children and families and to preserve the history and memory of Harriet Tubman by offering the general public an interpretive history of her achievements. This mission includes acting as an advocate for the children, youth and families and promoting historical preservation.

—"About Us," Harriet Tubman Organization website, http://htorganization. blogspot.com/p/blog-page.html

OPPOSITE, TOP: The late Donald Pinder and Ruth Braxton, Harriet Tubman Organization. *Charlie Ewers.*

OPPOSITE, BOTTOM: Bazel's Methodist Episcopal Church, where annual Harriet Tubman Day observances were held at least as early as 1967. The Harriet Tubman poster found in the pulpit there in 1963, however, suggests that other commemorations were held there as far back as the 1940s. *Charlie Ewers.*

A descendant of Harriet Tubman, Mrs. Addie Clash Travers organized the first Harriet Tubman Day in 1967 at Bazzel [*sic*] Church. In 1983 she helped organize the Harriet Tubman Organization....She served as their president for many years and also was a narrator for groups visiting Harriet Tubman's birthplace.

—Addie C. Travers obituary, (Easton) *Star-Democrat*, January 26, 1994

The Harriet Tubman Organization will hold its annual Harriet Tubman Day Annual Celebration, Saturday, March 10....The first Harriet Tubman Day Celebration began several decades ago by Addie Clash Travers in June. Now the celebration is held to coincide with March 10, the date Harriet Tubman died in Auburn, NY.

—*Dorchester Star*, "Saturday Celebrate Harriet Tubman Day," March 9, 2007

"The National Park Service is not going to do the research," [John] Creighton said. "We've got to produce information."

—Gail Dean, "Many Details of Tubman's Life Remain Buried in History," (Easton) *Star-Democrat*, July 30, 2002

Pinning down actual places associated with Tubman's life is one of the goals of the Harriet Tubman Organization History Discussion Group. It is also becoming more important to the future of any effort to memorialize the Moses of her people in the county of her birth....

The most recent discussion...focused on 18 historic sites associated with Harriet Tubman.

John Creighton, who offered this collection of research, began the discussion by explaining that these places "possibly, possibly, maybe" were associated with Tubman's life.

—Gail Dean, "Many Details of Tubman's Life Remain Buried in History," (Easton) *Star-Democrat*, July 30, 2002

Harriet Tubman is someone anybody would consider a hero.

—Wini Roche, Dorchester director of tourism, in Mark K. Sanders, "In Dorchester County, Tubman Is Tops," (Salisbury) *Daily Times*, February 5, 1996

It's not a black thing. It's not a white thing. It's just people.

—Reverend Linda Wheatley, in Gail Dean, "Community Day Stresses Unity," (Easton) *Star-Democrat*, September 11, 1992

"John [Creighton] will always be someone special to our family," said Tubman-Ross family representative Patricia Ross-Tubman. "He showed everyone how important our family legacy is. Our family is extremely grateful to John and his devotion to telling the story of our family."

—John Holt, "Creighton Remembered for Harriet Tubman Works," *Dorchester Star*, September 16, 2016

Charlie Ewers.

John Creighton. You really should mention him.

—Shirley Jackson, trustee,
Harriet Tubman Organization

John Creighton had meetings. He found information about my family. About Joseph Griffith in 1901 and John Griffith, who had land.

—Bertha Mack, trustee,
Harriet Tubman Organization

Charlie Ewers.

Charlie Ewers.

I became involved through John Creighton. I knew Evelyn Townsend. After sessions with John Creighton, I wanted to know more. I began to trace my ancestors. I did what I could do here— encouraging tours and talking.

—William Jarmon, trustee,
Harriet Tubman Organization

Harriet began to move back to Dorchester County. The lady is here....She's telling you, "I'm here, and I'm here to stay."

—Valerie Ross Manokey, in Gail Dean, "New Tubman Painting Unveiled in Cambridge," (Easton) *Star-Democrat*, July 27, 2011

Tubman's portrait was unveiled Thursday by dignitaries, including Charles Ross, the Cambridge artist who created not one, but two paintings here. He is a relative of Tubman's....

The artist was often joined by visitors as he worked on the painting earlier this summer. "I've seen people here crying," [Valerie Ross] Manokey said, explaining how watching the painting develop was like watching Harriet Tubman come back to life....

The State Highway Association created the Harriet Tubman Memorial Garden on property it owns adjacent to U.S. Route 50 [in 2001] after the Dorchester stretch of the interstate was dedicated to Tubman's memory in 1997.

—Gail Dean, "New Tubman Painting," 2011

The City of Cambridge and Dorchester County Tourism dedicated the county's newest mural Friday, July 21....

The mural...highlights Cambridge's African American history, culture and heritage....

At the center of the mural is Harriet Tubman, a Dorchester County native and conductor of the Underground Railroad. To her right is Gloria Richardson Dandridge, a key figure of the civil rights movement in Cambridge in the 1960s.

—Dustin Holt, "Mural Celebrates African American Heritage," (Easton) *Star-Democrat*, July 30, 2017

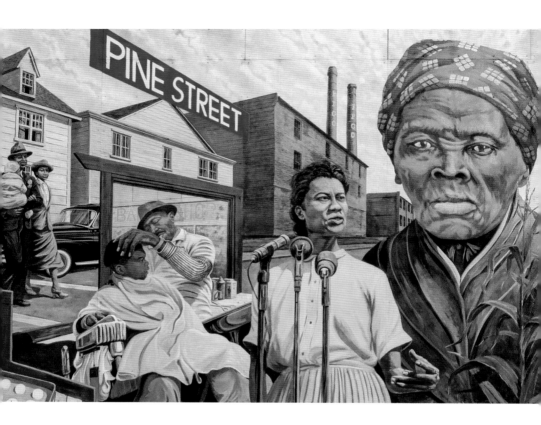

I set out to represent Harriet Tubman as a strong but compassionate woman that would be staring at you the viewer and offering her hand to take you on the journey to freedom. I wanted this image to project all the traits that made this iconic woman a hero to her people and an inspiration to all who will be viewing it.

—artist Michael Rosato, in Byron Dobson, "In Artistic Awe," *Tallahassee Democrat*, May 28, 2019

ABOVE: The "Local African-American Heritage Mural" on Ocean Gateway (U.S. Highway 50) with Harriet Tubman featured in the center was completed in 2017 by Michael Rosato, who also painted the Harriet Tubman mural next to the Harriet Tubman Organization building on Race Street. *Charlie Ewers.*

FOLLOWING: Michael Rosato, *Take My Hand*, the 2019 Harriet Tubman mural at 424 Race Street, Cambridge. The compelling image has been the backdrop of many selfies and facebook postings, notably a picture of three-year-old Lovie Hope Duncan giving a high-five to Tubman's outstretched hand, which went viral, being shared twenty thousand times in two weeks. According to Byron Dobson of the *Tallahassee Democrat*, the portrait of Harriet Tubman has "a look on her face that seems to say, 'trust me, you can do this.'" *Charlie Ewers.*

©M.R

Harriet Tubman's contributions to our state transcend race, gender, nationality, and religion, and her legacy continues to inspire us to this day....As a state and as a nation, we have come a long way from the days when Harriet Tubman walked these very lands. But here in Maryland, we will never forget that we owe much of that progress to trailblazers like Harriet Tubman, who paved the way for so many others.

—Governor Larry Hogan, in Victoria Wingate, "Harriet Tubman Underground Railroad Visitor Center Opens," (Denton) *Times-Record*, March 15, 2017

ABOVE: The March 10, 2017 ribbon-cutting at the Harriet Tubman Underground Railroad State Park, including (*left to right*): Maryland National Parks Superintendent Mary Settina, Maryland Treasurer Nancy Kopp, U.S. Senator Ben Cardin, Senator Addie Eckardt, Comptroller Peter Franchot, Governor Larry Hogan, Harriet Tubman reenactor Millicent Sparks, Lieutenant Governor Boyd Rutherford, National Parks Service Northeast Regional Deputy Director Rose Fennell and Dorchester County Council President Ricky Travers. *Maryland Department of National Resources.*

By studying Harriet Tubman, I fell in love with the landscape. Where she was born. Where she worked as a child. I have walked some of the trails at Blackwater. But changes have taken place. Look at what was the marsh around the Little Blackwater.

—William Jarmon, trustee, Harriet Tubman Organization

Bertha Mack, Harriet Tubman Organization. *Charlie Ewers.*

People can't leave without taking something back home that will stay. They will take something back that they will cherish. They are more excited than us, because we live with it. By coming here, they can touch and walk on the ground she walked upon. They will certainly come back.

—Bertha Mack, trustee, Harriet Tubman Organization

Charlie Ewers.

It may be difficult to imagine the brutality of Harriet Tubman's early life, but it is possible for all of us to appreciate her connection to the land here in Dorchester County. Having spent a lot of my time as a youngster on a Dorchester farm, I can feel her relationship with the land. I believe that those who view the [African American heritage] mural will see the same connection between Harriet Tubman and the land of her birth and the people who came after and surround her here.

—Amanda Fenstermaker, director of tourism, Dorchester County

When people take a tour of Harriet Tubman's native land, they can touch and feel the sites that she would have touched. People want to get off the bus at the Brodess Farm to walk on sacred ground. Why can't we go to her birthplace? Maybe we can do so in the future. But you can see the area. You can see the store. You can see where her mother was born on Kentuck Swamp Road and imagine her getting from one place to another on Indian trails.

—William Jarmon, trustee, Harriet Tubman Organization

Charlie Ewers.

narratives to find commonalities and eventually a way forward. This sounds a lot like the dictum from Chaim Perelman and Lucie Olbrechts-Tyteca in my own academic field of rhetoric, that the first step in reaching agreement between disputing parties is to find *some* common ground, no matter how small.

Our book project, *A Guide to Harriet Tubman's Eastern Shore: The Old Home Is Not There*, has been an attempt on our part to tell the stories of both a shared space—the *literal* common ground of Dorchester County, Maryland—and the human communities who have shared it from the time of Harriet Tubman up to the present. We are hoping the narratives that result will enable people of goodwill to discover bridges not only into our shared history but also between communities.

The subtitle chosen for this book comes from a story attributed to Harriet Tubman about a man who was released after serving a twenty-five-year prison term: "He leaves the prison gates, he makes his way to his old home, but his old home is not there," she said. "So it was with me."

That story resonates with me as well. I have not been imprisoned, neither I nor my ancestors have been enslaved and I was not, like Harriet Tubman, born on the Eastern Shore, but I did live and work here forty-some years ago, and as Dana Paterra says in the Afterword about Tubman's experiences retold in *The View North* exhibit at the Visitor Center, I've been "brought back…again and again." Now I've returned, permanently I hope, after a few of what Dana calls "rough patches," and it's pretty clear that in a number of ways, "the old home is not there."

The first house I ever owned was in the Newtown district of Salisbury. Like many houses in that neighborhood in those days, the huge American Foursquare structure was, as a realtor friend of ours would put it, "severely cosmetically challenged." But that made it cheap enough for a poorly paid teacher to afford, and with my young man's enthusiasm (read naiveté) I thought I could restore it in no time. Five years later, the house had fresh paint, new insulation and way too much of the then-popular plywood paneling over its cracked plaster, and I had some newfound carpentry skills to kickstart my career as a contractor.

Twenty-some years later, after living and working in a lot of places from Baltimore to Wisconsin and back, my wife and I bought a house in Rumbley, Somerset County, where we spent weekends and summer vacations and learned on trips to Salisbury that my former home was in a way "not there," having become nearly unrecognizable due to neglected maintenance, even though the neighborhood in general was looking up.

And we learned in Rumbley a more literal meaning for "not there," as rising water levels over the years turned larger and larger pieces of our property into marsh. By the time we sold that house so that I could go to graduate school and eventually land a professorship in the mountains of Western Maryland, flooding at high tide had become commonplace, and we had a lot more *Spartina* growing in the yard than lawn grass and dandelions.

Fast-forward another twenty years to the present, and we have again been drawn back to the Shore; such is the nature of this place. We now live on (fairly) high ground, in an old house that has been (kind of) well maintained, but both of those other old homes are nearing the point of no return: the porch is falling off the poor Salisbury house, and the Rumbley house has apparently been abandoned to the marsh, both bearing witness to the rot that can overtake structures—and also history—in the steamy Eastern Shore climate when caretaking fails.

ABOVE: The coauthor's former home in Rumbley, apparently abandoned to the marsh. *Charlie Ewers.*

ABOVE: Dying loblolly ghost forest in Dorchester County. *Charlie Ewers.*

OPPOSITE: An old Eastern Shore house shows what years of neglect can do. *Charlie Ewers.*

Finally, consider this map of roughly the same area from the U.S. Fish & Wildlife Service. All of the area in blue is projected to be under water in less than eighty years from now:

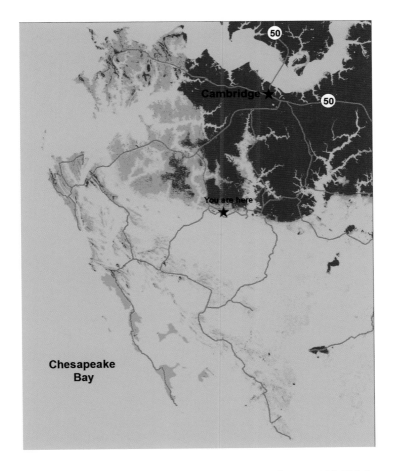

Sea Level Affecting Marshes Model (SLAMM) simulation for 2100. *U.S. Fish & Wildlife Service.*

One example of the effect of climate change on the lands Harriet Tubman would have known can be found in the recently discovered cabin site of her father, Ben Ross, which has already become more accessible by water than by land. Note the reason for the purchase of the site by the federal government, as reported in *Bay Journal* (emphasis mine):

> *Maryland and federal officials announced...that a state archaeological team uncovered a trove of artifacts at the site believed to be where Tubman's father, Ben Ross, had lived in a cabin during his enslavement and which he owned outright as a free man by the 1840s.*
>
> *The site was found on a 2,600-acre tract that the U.S. Fish and Wildlife Service bought last year on Peters Neck, a mostly wooded peninsula southwest of Cambridge. It was purchased for $6 million* to give the extensive marsh at the Blackwater refuge room to migrate inland as climate change raises sea level around the Chesapeake Bay.

As Harriet Tubman's native landscape inexorably disappears, we need to keep in mind that multiple human communities have shared this landscape ever since European settlers arrived. We must also acknowledge that the particular *way* in which the resources of this landscape have been exploited has contributed to their dwindling as much as the rising tides. In the words of Wendell Berry,

> *The white race in America has marketed and destroyed more of the fertility of the earth in less time than any other race that ever lived. In* [the places where slavery existed] *at least, this is largely to be accounted for by the racial division of the* experience *of the landscape. The white man, preoccupied with the abstractions of the economic exploitation and ownership of the land, necessarily has lived on the country as a destructive force, an ecological catastrophe, because he assigned the hand labor, and in that the possibility of intimate knowledge of the land, to a people he considered racially inferior; in thus debasing labor, he destroyed the possibility of meaningful contact with the earth....Because he did not know the land, it was inevitable that he would squander its natural bounty, deplete its richness, corrupt and pollute it, or destroy it altogether.*[2]

2. *The Hidden Wound,* 105.

Thankfully, the Dorchester landscape, while sorely depleted, has not yet been completely destroyed, and the fact that diverse communities of people can still share that landscape and make a living from what remains of its bounty is worthy of celebration.

We can celebrate the continued, resilient beauty of this land, both in its wild places and in its still-productive forests and cropland, as seen here on the site of the Brodess Farm where Harriet Tubman worked.

And we can also celebrate the preservation and commemoration efforts that allow current communities to have bridges to the past, such as this new mural on the wall of the Harriet Tubman Organization's Cambridge office—on the very same Race Street that I referred to at the beginning of these reflections.

PREVIOUS: Field and forest, Brodess Farm Site. *Charlie Ewers.*

ABOVE: New Harriet Tubman mural at 424 Race Street, Cambridge. *Charlie Ewers.*

We have photographed and interviewed people whose narratives still reveal tensions between communities—Black residents remembering, for example, being treated in the basement of the Cambridge hospital (if at all) and the constant fear of lynching, and some white residents wondering why everybody's making such a fuss over a Black woman who "stole property" (the slaves she helped to escape) or doubting that she had the navigational skills necessary to lead people on the section of the Underground Railroad from Dorchester to Pennsylvania.

But most of the individuals we have encountered in the course of this project are vibrant and committed people, proud of their Eastern Shore roots and determined to preserve memories of the past—the horrors along with the beauties—but equally determined not to live in that past. Following the spirit of Harriet Tubman, these women and men have taken on the mission of leading their communities into a brighter future, whether by providing legal advocacy or helping a child with her *Junior Ranger Activity Book*, saving a historic store or shepherding a congregation, logging and trapping responsibly or running a revitalized city.

Phil and I are immensely grateful to all these folks, Black and white, older and younger, who made time to share their visions with us. We hope that this book helps our readers, and people of goodwill all over the Shore, to discover bridges into our shared history and to find in Harriet Tubman's example strong, sure guidance for the road ahead.

—CHARLIE EWERS

Afterword

T he Harriet Tubman Underground Railroad Visitor Center broke ground on the 100th anniversary of Harriet Tubman's death in March 2013 and opened to the public four years later in March 2017. The design concept for the park, *The View North*, symbolizes the journey of a freedom seeker to better their circumstances. The two main structures, the Visitor Center and Administration Building, are situated on a south–north axis framing an open and welcoming area to the north. The experience begins as you enter in the southernmost portion of the park, and the journey continues as you move northward. The entrance

Charlie Ewers.

and southernmost pavilion of the exhibit building are clad in cedar, a tree common on Maryland's Eastern Shore. There you will find modern-day amenities such as the information desk, restrooms and store. As you move north to the exhibits in the three pavilions clad in zinc, you are immersing yourself in Harriet Tubman's world and making your way north toward freedom.

You begin your journey north with Harriet Tubman learning how faith, family and community challenged the brutality of slavery. You learn how

Harriet was put to work, trapping muskrats as a child and cutting and hauling timber as an adult. You understand her connections to the landscape where she spent her formative years and learned survival skills that contributed to her successful rescue missions. You also see how relationships with free African Americans formed communication networks that linked free and enslaved people and helped to nourish a vision of freedom in the North as well as provide important resources to freedom seekers.

Through the exhibits, you make your way north along the Underground Railroad. You learn that it was a resistance movement and not a *physical* railroad and also that Tubman did not start the Underground Railroad. She utilized the important connections and resources the Underground Railroad provided and came into prominence by bringing others to freedom along its many routes.

As you complete your voyage to the northernmost pavilion and begin to return south again, you view exhibits that pay tribute to Tubman's accomplishments later in life, including her numerous roles in the Civil War and her work as a suffragist and humanitarian. Harriet Tubman's life and legacy tell us that regardless of your disadvantages you can make decisions that have a positive effect on others. Tubman shows us that ordinary people can do extraordinary things.

For me, the story of *The View North* here is also a story about love. Love of her family brought her back again and again to the Eastern Shore of Maryland. She wanted her family members to be safe with her. This is a universal concept that we can all relate to.

Whenever in my life I journey through a "rough patch," I take heart in how Harriet Tubman was determined and courageous. She inspires me to give 110 percent of my efforts every day.

When you visit Harriet Tubman Underground Railroad Visitor Center, stand by the glass windows. Sit on the bench by her statue. Reflect on the accomplishments of her life. You are sure to agree with me that you have made an intense odyssey—a journey that fills you with the positivity of Harriet Tubman's faith, love and vision.

—DANA PATERRA
Park Manager, Harriet Tubman Underground Railroad State Park

Index

S

selling South (enslaved people) 10, 13, 50, 214, 234
Smith, Seba 228
songs (antislavery) 240–241, 255
SS *Harriet Tubman* 268, 269, 270
steamboats 62, 65, 67, 193, 239, 246, 247, 248, 251, 262
Stewart family
  James A. 43, 140
  John T. 43, 140, 143, 145, 147
Stewart's Canal 14, 22, 56, 65, 66, 69, 81, 137, 139, 147
Still, William 169, 174, 176, 230, 232, 245
Stowe, Harriet Beecher 140
Stump, Brice 40, 52, 53, 264, 284, 287

T

timber industry 145, 147, 148, 156
Tobacco Stick. *See* Madison
Townsend, Evelyn 292
Trapping 107, 109, 110
Trinity Methodist Episcopal Church (New Hughes M.E. Church) 181
Tubman biographers
  Adams, Samuel Hopkins 54, 55, 56, 115, 205, 224, 240
  Bradford, Sarah Hopkins passim
  Cheney, Ednah Dow 112, 134, 160, 169, 222, 226, 245
  Conrad, Earl 266, 270
  Dennis, Charles 214, 220
  Drake, Frank C. 84, 202, 206, 244
  Garrett, Thomas 230, 246, 247, 251, 259
  Mason, James E. 160
  Sanborn, Franklin B. 84, 102, 107, 120, 126, 130, 133, 139, 140, 148, 150, 202, 229

Tatlock, Helen Woodruff 257
Taylor, Robert W. 133, 259
Telford, Emma Paddock 79, 87, 88, 90, 92, 93, 100, 120, 129, 130, 188, 247, 256, 257
Wyman, Lillie B. Chace 82, 133, 233, 247
Tubman, Harriet
  ability to disguise herself 206
  healing and nursing 204, 205
  ruses 247, 256, 257
  singing 206, 246
  special powers 198, 199, 202
  spirituality 160, 207, 208
  use of medical herbs 204, 205
  visions 202, 204
Turner, Nat 171, 172, 173

U

Underground Railroad
  general 242, 243
  strategies 226, 228

W

Washington, Booker T. 244
weaving 102, 103, 104, 105, 106, 126
White, Dinez 278, 282
Wilson, Robert 43
Wingate, P.J. 39
worship, African American 166, 168, 170, 171, 175, 178, 187, 188
WPA "Slave Narratives"
  Anderson, Andy J. 106
  Bellus, Cyrus 103
  Birdsong, Nelson 92
  Clay, Henry 84
  Henson, Annie Young 166
  Jurdon, Lucindy Lawrence 102

About the Authors

Phillip Hesser is a lecturer and educator who has taught most recently at Salisbury University. His previous book is *What a River Says: Exploring the Blackwater River and Refuge* (Cambridge: Friends of Blackwater, 2014).

Charlie Ewers lives on the Eastern Shore of Maryland and teaches in the Environmental Studies Department of Salisbury University. His award-winning photographs are featured in galleries in Annapolis, Ocean City and Berlin.

Visit us at
www.historypress.com